# TRAUMA
## AND THE MYSTERY OF THE
# SUBCONSCIOUS.

### KABBALAH, OUR INNER MIND, AND HOW WE ALREADY HOLD THE SECRETS OF HEALING WITHIN OURSELVES.

*by David Dardashti*

RABBI, SCHOLAR, SCIENTIFIC RESEARCHER

# TABLE OF CONTENTS

# TRAUMA & THE MYSTERY OF THE SUBCONSCIOUS

## Kabbalah, our inner mind, and how we already hold the secrets to healing within ourselves.

### By Rabbi David Dardashti

*Ibogaine should only be administered by a seasoned practitioner with a long track record of successful treatments, and in a clinical context under medical supervision. Any treatments or protocols discussed in this book, refer to the use only of 99.9% pure ibogaine, in a rigorously controlled environment by professionals, with both medical and therapeutic expertise.

# FOREWORD

This book illustrates how to heal from trauma.

But to do so, we have to take a journey into that place that some consider science, and others consider spirituality.

You see, science and spirituality, for too many, are concepts that are in opposition.

One is rooted in the measurable observation of the natural world, and the other (many assume) is based solely in the teachings and dogma of organized religions.

This is simply untrue.

It is a misconception, and one that this book hopes to put a stop to, not for any theological purpose, but as a part of the journey toward understanding the human mind/spirit connection, and how it's crucial to activating our potential to heal, grow, and achieve.

At the heart of this book, we will dive into parts of our mind most of us do not even consider on an average day. But as we do, we will illustrate our inner mind's capabilities for healing, and highlight its connection to the more ethereal elements of our existence: the soul, human interconnection, and forces greater than ourselves.

We will show how, through science and spirituality combined, we are able to heal our own psyches.

As a framework for this, we will reference often the Kabbalah. What is Kabbalah? Well, it's the closest thing we as humans have access to in terms of a 'science', but one that focuses on including the elements *beyond* our measurable physical world. Not just the parts of the universe that we *see*, but the parts we *feel*.

It is here, in this space between the physical body and the spiritual self, where we can find the root of issues like trauma, addiction, and depression.

In essence, this is where the subconscious lives, permanently a part of us, but a window into a world far beyond our body's flesh and bone boundaries. Humanity is still only scratching the surface of its capabilities, but in this book, we use every tool at our disposal to investigate and understand how we can harness it to heal.

And we're in good company. When thinkers like Karl Jung and Isaac Newton wanted to delve deeper into the realm of the subconscious, they turned to Kabbalah, as we'll see in more detail later.

Renowned for their almost preternatural contributions to the spheres of the human mind and science, they knew their knowledge still paled in comparison to what was left to learn.

It is in this spirit we venture forward in this book, with the desire to speak with harmony between the worlds of science and spirituality.

# 1. TRAUMA, AND THE MYSTERY OF THE SUBCONSCIOUS

Have you ever wondered why certain things scare you? Why a simple noise in the middle of the day might frighten you in a way you never expected? Why some memories just pop up out of nowhere? Or why you feel sad sometimes without any reason? Well, you're not alone.

These questions puzzle many of us, and the answers often lie in a place we can't usually see, and certainly don't usually think about – our subconscious mind.

What is the subconscious?

Imagine your mind is like an iceberg. The part above the water is everything you're aware of right now – your conscious mind. But below the water, that huge part of the iceberg you can't see, that's your subconscious. It's a vast and mysterious place that holds all your past experiences, feelings, and thoughts that you're not actively thinking about.

What is trauma, and how does it hide in the subconscious?

Trauma is a kind of injury, but not like a cut on your knee. It's an emotional wound that can happen when you go through something very dramatic, from extreme experiences such as war or violence, to more commonplace situations like a bad accident, losing someone close to you, or even two parents fighting in front of a child. These experiences can be so painful that your mind wants to forget them, so it pushes them down into your subconscious. But just because you're not thinking about them doesn't mean they're gone.

They can still affect how you feel and act without you even realizing it.

How have we traditionally viewed trauma?

In Western countries, people used to not talk much about emotional wounds. It was like if you couldn't see the injury, it wasn't there. But over time, doctors and scientists started to understand that trauma is real and it can really mess with your head and your heart. They saw how soldiers coming back from war were struggling and how kids who had been through hard times were having a difficult time adapting. So, they began to take it seriously and look for ways to help. But it hasn't always been so easy.

## What's the truth about trauma and the subconscious?

The truth is, trauma and the subconscious are very old friends. When something traumatic happens, it often slips into the subconscious, where it can stay hidden for a long time. It's like when you put something in a safe and forget the combination. It's still there, but you can't get to it. That's why sometimes you might feel scared or sad and not know why – because of the trauma locked away in your subconscious. In the next few pages we'll explain in detail what exactly trauma is, and how the body processes it.

What does this book want to do?

This book has a big and important job. It aims to shine a light on how trauma and the subconscious are connected. It's like giving you the combination to the safe so you can open it and see what's inside. And it's not just about understanding it; it's about healing from it.

In this book, we will share the reality of what we discovered after 15 years of experience and healing over and 250 individuals with severe traumas - that there is absolutely a solution and it involves what we know will become the most important substance you may never have heard of, a natural substance called ibogaine, which we will talk about in detail in the coming chapters.

**Why this book, and why now?**

Contemporary medicine has come a long way. but along with the great improvements in lifespan, and the elimination of many common illnesses, has come an increase in challenges like depression, addiction, increased suicide rates, and the degradation of families.

We can think of these as the 'ailments of the modern age'. Think about it: while our bodies have been getting more resistant thanks to Western medicine, our minds, and our souls, still have a lot of ground to cover.

Sometimes it feels as if we're doing ok at functioning, but increasingly, we're having trouble with thriving.

Some of the reasons are widely known, if not always defined clearly. What are they? Some feel the weight of social media, the constant stream of negativity or shallow entertainment, another, is the deterioration of meaningful social connection, and yet another, the fact that it's so easy to distract ourselves from what's happening inside ourselves as individuals.

We convince ourselves that there must be nothing broken inside, because we simply have no time to self-assess, isn't that correct?

For this reason, this book has an urgency to it. We hope this book can be a moment to step back, think about our own suffering that we hide inside, and come away with a true understanding of what we can do to move forward.

But first, while we have total confidence in our mission and info here, we are not alone in our efforts to shed light on trauma, and so we must take a moment to pay respects to all the hardworking Pioneers of Trauma Treatment.

While the solutions to trauma outlined in this book are completely unique, and can truly and permanently help, the quest to understand and heal trauma has spanned centuries and been the collective undertaking of countless dedicated professionals across various fields.

It's upon this vast wealth of knowledge, research, and compassionate care that we now build our understanding of ibogaine's potential. Before diving deeper into the world of ibogaine, it's essential we pay our respects and show heartfelt appreciation for all those who have paved the way.

The realm of trauma treatment is vast. Psychotherapists dedicate years, sometimes even their entire lives, delving into the intricate layers of the human psyche, helping individuals reconcile with their pasts.

Their patience and perseverance often unravel the profound depths of human suffering, enabling countless individuals to find a semblance of peace. Similarly, medical doctors, researchers, and scientists have toiled tirelessly to understand the biochemical and neurological intricacies of trauma. Their findings have shaped policies, informed therapeutic methodologies, and provided hope to millions.

They've offered solace in the form of therapy sessions, developed medications, and initiated community outreach programs, all with the singular goal of alleviating human suffering.

Rehabilitation centers, with their structured programs, have offered sanctuary to those grappling with the chains of addiction. The relentless commitment of their staff, from counselors to caregivers, has illuminated pathways of recovery for countless souls otherwise lost in the dark alleys of dependency.

Also, it's crucial to recognize the role of pharmaceutical innovations. While it's true that certain medications have unfortunately contributed to addiction crises, many pharmaceutical interventions have been nothing short of lifesaving. Medications have stabilized moods, reduced the debilitating symptoms of post-traumatic stress, and offered a bridge to recovery for many.

Yet, in every field, there's always room for innovation, for new insights that can further enhance our understanding and treatment methodologies. This is where ibogaine enters the narrative. Not as a replacement for these monumental efforts, but as a potential addition, a new tool in our ever-evolving toolkit to combat trauma and addiction.

Drawing inspiration from the vast repository of knowledge that has come before, along with over 15 years of our own intense research alongside psychiatrists, therapists, and medical doctors, ibogaine therapy can offer a relatively rapid, intensive therapeutic experience. But, the properties of ibogaine alone are not enough to truly heal an individual, so it is the combination of ibogaine's neurological properties on top of the vast history of research on trauma, a skilled practitioner's hand, and over 35 years of study of the Kabballah, and its deep understanding of the subconscious.

It is with respect for all these predecessors in the realm of trauma and addiction treatment that we have been able to delve into and unlock the potential of ibogaine. Every advancement, every breakthrough is a testament to humanity's collective endeavor to heal and thrive.

## The Truth About Trauma and How to Heal from It.

Along with understanding how ibogaine can act as a catalyst: we will do two things in this book: first, to show how trauma shapes our society, and second, to offer a clear path to healing. We'll share stories from over 15 years of helping clients, stories that show how deep the roots of trauma can go. But we're not just here to tell stories. We're here to change the conversation about trauma.

We need to talk about our past in a new way. It starts with understanding what trauma really is. We'll give you a clear picture of trauma, showing how it touches people from all walks of life. And we'll talk about how it changes us, how it's a part of our development as people, but, in an ideal world, shouldn't cloud that ability to develop and move forward.

But we won't stop at just talking about trauma. We'll show, in very clear terms, how to uproot it, how to fix it, and how to heal. We've spent 35 years studying the subconscious, natural medicine, and healing. We've developed over 300 ways to find and heal deep traumas. And we'll share how we can work with the subconscious to help the body heal *itself*.

Trauma might seem complicated, but it's also simple. It's part of life, but it doesn't have to control life. There is hope. Healing is possible.

In this book, we'll explore what trauma means to different people. We'll show you how to spot it and how to heal from it. And we'll show you how to break free from trauma for good.

What can trauma do to us?

The word "trauma" is everywhere these days. The world feels smaller, and we hear about bad things all the time. News is full of wars, abuse, and disaster. And some people use "trauma" to describe anything that feels even minimally dramatic.

But trauma is a real challenge, especially for modern medicine. In the U.S., a lot of mental health care is about medicine that helps you feel better – the challenge is, this doesn't usually cure the root problem. And where there is severe trauma, it's even more difficult. If you don't get it out, it spreads like a disease.

Ultimately, trauma is both simpler than people might realize, while being more complexly integrated into how we evolve and mature as people.

Through the course of this book, we'll explore the ways people define trauma, the clearest way to identify it, and the astonishing advancements in the way individuals can be free from it, through unique methods we have developed, to penetrate deeper layers of the Subconscious and achieve complete freedom from torturous recorded trauma forever.

*Trauma: the remnants of a*
*deeply distressing or disturbing*
*experience*

Before we go any further, it is our duty to carefully define trauma, as we have seen it, through thousands of consultations. And not just that, but make the definition so crystal clear, that it becomes obviously how we must look at it as a society.

With shocking consistency from the individuals we have helped, we can simply and with complete confidence, define it as such:

A traumatic experience occurs for an individual, is processed in that moment through the conscious mind and senses, and then is stored in the subconscious, put away for the conscious mind to be able to continue the daily survival of the organism.

Let's call the complete trauma a picture or a painting, the full frame tucked away in the warehouse of our subconscious. All the details, memories and imagery associated with this event are indeed stored, but simply repressed and not available to our waking consciousness.

Rather, only pieces of this event, fragments of the occurrence, remain accessible to our conscious. We catch glimpses of the suppressed memory, and our brain struggles to complete the pictures, but all we have is a few fragments, like stray puzzle pieces, to work from.

As time goes by, and the trauma continues unprocessed, this disconnect between the perception of the full event, and the daily reality of the person's consciousness, means the mind continues to search for the complete picture, seeing only fragments every day.

In essence, the conscious mind knows there is something missing, knows there is a hole in the psyche, and is in a constant struggle trying to understand.

Now, depending on the severity of the original trauma, or the individual's natural personality, support network, history of therapy or other tools to process their past, we can see a host of effects. We will, of course, go into that further in subsequent chapters, but this desire to 'fill the hole' so to speak, is at the root of the undesired anxiety and depression, to unwanted behaviors like substance abuse or personality problems.

With this definition clear, we can continue digging into how the power of the mind is at the heart of both the challenges of trauma, and the power to heal from it.

The word "trauma" has become a frequently used word in the past decade or so. There are several reasons for this.

First, the smaller the world has become due to greater social and technological connectivity, the more we hear and read about tragedies, like the horrors of war, claims of tremendous abuse and general ill-treatment.

This is especially so as the news organizations have increasingly made tragedy, disaster and perceived abuse as the main part of the news cycle.

Second, in cultures where victimization is a prominent mindset, there's a tendency for people, especially activists, to use the term loosely and apply it to anything that might be considered unjust.

Third, because of the above and the apparent increases in distressing and disturbing experiences, more focus has been given to the different forms of trauma and how they can be best treated.

In some ways, the treatment of trauma, represents a serious and persistent challenge to modern medicine. In many modern healthcare systems, especially in the U.S., much of healthcare, especially mental healthcare, takes the form of medication that doesn't provide a cure, but rather symptomatic relief.

Such medicine can, in some cases and in some disorders, re-establish a person's functionality making it a useful tool.

However, trauma is different. Unless successfully extracted from the mind-body, trauma not only doesn't go away, it actually can get worse. The emotional discomfort not only stays around, it gets imprinted on to many other experiences. In that sense, trauma can be like a cancer – it spreads.

Trauma also tells us a lot about the mind, body, consciousness and the subconscious.

During the early days of psychiatry, the conscious and subconscious were considered simply as different parts of the mind – the omnipotent mind that controlled everything. Over time and with better understanding of the mind-body connection, it became apparent that this early definition of medical psychiatry was too simplistic so that eventually, Candace Pert, a leader in neuroscience research, was able in 1995 to announce with confidence that "the body is the subconscious."

With this simple statement, Pert successfully brought to light the concept that the subconscious is not only 'part' of the body, but its very essence. It touches not only every cell in the body, but moves beyond the body into the spiritual and ethereal realm.

Pert's research and that of many others over the last three decades has shown the mind-body is indeed an amazingly complex system of trillions of interconnected cells that are constantly processing our worlds, at the rate of 11 million bits per second, and from this flood of info, it constantly presents perceptions and suggestions to our consciousness.

And often consciousness simply accepts these notions, often with no thought at all. Because these pieces of information come from within our own mind, our consciousness will often assume that we have all the info we need and accept certain notions as complete truth. Often, what we believe to be the truth about our own past, isn't, especially when we are in a traumatized state.

A simple example, is the well-known concept of how a child might blame themselves for their parents' divorce. This result is so well known in psychology, that many parents *do* know that they should make sure their child doesn't feel guilty. However, in the mind of a child who did not receive this reassurance, they can very well grow and live the rest of their lives believing their guilt to be absolutely true.

In this book, I will reveal what I have found out in the past twenty years consulting with hundreds of people with trauma, and decades more studying Kabbalah and the human spirit, and show what are the successful elements to healing.

It is my hope that this will help enlighten both those who suffer from trauma and those who are in the business of treating it to recognize that there are indeed successful solutions for a condition that affects millions of people: solutions that expunge the trauma rather than burying it deeper into the soul.

## Understanding in Detail the Effects of Trauma

Now that we've understood exactly what trauma is in the simplest way possible, what are the results of its persistence in our society? It is our duty to explain how trauma can create very specific effects, many of which are very long-lasting. In fact, they can potentially influence the entire trajectory of a person's life and their families. There are numerous reasons for this.

Just like a virus that can linger for years unless expunged from the body, trauma in its many facets not only lingers in the past but imprints itself on the present, perpetuating a toxic scenario that threatens to affect every aspect of a person's psyche.

The unprocessed and unresolved trauma exists like a ticking time bomb waiting to explode when the circumstances align themselves to form a critical mass that can trigger disaster.

Trauma awaits, locked safely away in the subconscious and protected by a self-destructive reluctance to seek it out and destroy it.

The fear of fear is one of the great reasons why trauma can successfully hide from the light of exposure.

What is now a commonly known Winston Churchill quote, is perhaps nowhere more evident than in this very topic of trauma. For many people, their recollection and understanding of personal horrors is massively hindered by the fear that their fate is worse than they could possibly imagine, or worse than anyone else's.

The anxiety that their trauma is unimaginable, is what makes it unimaginable. Not just unimaginable, but never exposed.

The difficulty is that it is definitely possible to imagine something horrific happening to you that has never happened to you. You could probably imagine falling off a cliff, or being trapped by fire if it has never happened. However, once it has happened, that recall of trauma sets off a seismic emotional reaction that resonates throughout the mind-body and inspires only one action – total escape from the moment.

There's a big difference between your imagination and your memory. And your mind and body can *feel* the difference. This is why it is often easier for the mind to present these repressed images through dreams or nightmares, which are often completely startling to the trauma victim. They wake up, feel horrible effects of the dream's imagery, but are forced to continue their daily lives without fully understanding what the dreams mean.

Hebrew has a term 'Chalomot Shav Yedaberu', which means that dreams essentially have no meaning to our practical lives. Sure, some elements of some dreams may be based on things we feel or have experienced in our lives, but to spend too much time analyzing them or worrying over them simply has no value. Now, in the case that a person cannot simply ignore their dreams or nightmares, there is a further technique. In order to prevent this torment, the Kabbalah tell us to fast from dusk till dawn, as a protective way of replacing, with the physical challenge of hunger, the perception of a wrong act we may have committed, or the possibility that we may dwell and obsess over the dream.

And this is how the inherent qualities of trauma allow it to be hidden. That's how for many people, their past experiences remain just out of sight, an ill-formed and potentially horrific figure invisibly but always stalking your mind.

Faced with this challenge, most people just want to run.

Run away from the thoughts, run away from the feelings, run away from themselves. It's just too difficult.

Escape is always proportional to the threat. Just a little upset? Take a nap, meditate, go out for a walk.

Terrified about what secrets linger in your soul? Drink yourself into oblivion, drug yourself into another world, and try not to come back any time soon.

*Denial becomes the root action.*

"Anxiety" is often not a strong enough word to characterize this fear of fear. Sheer panic is closer to the truth; a crazed obsession to escape the horror. If survival is the main goal of the mind and body then it feels imperative to flee the horror and find safety, even if it comes in the most unsafe of forms such as substance abuse, self-harm or other dangerous patterns.

This insistent and persistent dynamic naturally leads to addiction, where the use of substances of all sorts, from alcohol to fentanyl, from cannabis to sugar, appears to be a life-saving strategy.

In a meta-analysis by neuroscientist Simon Thege et al., (2017) showed that about a third of trauma victims sought help for treatment of addictive behaviors. The researchers conclude:

"Results provide some support for a positive association between exposure to interpersonal trauma exposure and subsequent addictive behaviors."

And more recently, other researchers have also suggested that addictions to activities, like sexual addiction and gambling, also become part of the coping repertoire of some trauma survivors.

This brings us to a mystery. Why do people suffer so much when the root of the trauma generally was out of their control? It's not as if they chose to be traumatized.

One problem is that traumatized people are often made to believe that their trauma was in their control and partly their doing by abusers who in many cases do have a massive influence on their victims.

Indeed, the abuser is likely to blame the victim for their treatment. Such doubt is also amplified when the victim feels completely out of control of the situation.

A sense of control is a fundamental part of wellbeing. Feeling out of control of anything, is likely to bring on feelings of inadequacy and self-blame and retribution. Ironically, the more out of control you feel, the more responsible you can feel for your helplessness.

One way of trying to exercise control if you can't control yourself, is to attempt to control others. Ironically, this can lead to bullying, abusing and traumatizing others as compensation for one's own sense of inadequacy. It is unfortunately not that uncommon for the abused to become abusers. We will cover this phenomenon further in a later chapter dedicated specifically to bullying.

It's time we took a deep dive into the topic, and show how bullying is not simply an 'unfortunate reality' of modern society, and something most people experience at some point in their lives, but an all-too-clear piece of evidence that unprocessed trauma, across generations, can and currently does ripple through our world in a consequential way.

*The rampant scourge of trauma:*
*Bullying.*

On April 4, 2013, 17-year-old Rehtaeh Parsons hanged herself at her home in Dartmouth, Nova Scotia. Her parents came home and called for medical help, but the hanging left her permanently vegetative. After days in hospital, the decision was finally made to switch off her life support and allow her to die peacefully.

The reason for Rehtaeh's suicide was apparent enough. In November 2011, she went to a party with a friend where she was reportedly drugged and subsequently raped by four teenage boys. Someone took a picture which was then distributed all over Rehtaeh's school leading her to being branded a "slut." This led to a relentless harassment campaign with Canadian federal police texts and Facebook messages asking for sex. Despite being reported to the RCMP, the investigation ended with the decision not to lay charges due to insufficient evidence.

Rehtaeh made repeated attempts to change schools but the harassment continued. She also had a nervous breakdown, including suicide threats, leading her to be hospitalized for five days in a local hospital though she was later released into her parents' care.

Within days of Rehtaeh's suicide, her parents went public demanding answers and accusing the RCMP, Canada's federal police, of failing their daughter. The international outcry forced the RCMP to reopen the case and eventually led to several of the now-adult boys being prosecuted for the distribution of child pornography. Her case has since inspired renewed anti-bullying initiatives across Canada.

Rehateah's sad case is an example of the extremes that bullying can lead to, but the reality is that bullying can happen everywhere, and it's always traumatic.

Unfortunately, something that has become so common across generations, is something that continuously is being shown to be one of the most known, and most evident effects of trauma, both nominal and severe.

Sadly, because of its prevalence, it's often overlooked as just an 'occupational hazard' of living in a society. We're somewhere between desensitized or baffled about how to address it.

The more I've consulted and heard people's stories about their own traumas, however, the more I've seen the truth about bullying: that it, as a symptom, is evidence of how much unaddressed trauma is coursing through the veins of our population.

Let's take a minute to look deeper into the accepted research about bullying.

*Defining Bullying*

Usually defined as "the use of force, coercion, hurtful teasing, or making threats to inflict verbal or physical abuse on others for the purpose of intimidation," there are four main types of bullying:

*Physical bullying*

Most people think of this when they hear the word "bullying." It refers to using physical intimidation tactics such as stealing, shoving, hitting, fighting, or intentional vandalism to intimidate people and establish a "pecking order" with the bullies on top and the victim at the bottom. Since this usually occurs in schools, prisons, or other settings where "snitching" is considered taboo, victims are rarely free to tell authorities about what happened without becoming even more isolated.

Victims can be targeted for various reasons, whether because they are physically different in some way, belong to a discriminated-against minority, or simply because they stand out for other reasons. While most commonly associated with male bullies, female bullies are not unknown. Physical bullying is also most likely to escalate over time and can lead to dangerous outcomes (suicide or physical violence.)

*Verbal bullying*

Whether occurring along with physical bullying (or instead of it), verbal bullying can be just as traumatic. This can include name-calling or assigning an offensive nickname to someone, spreading malicious rumors, verbally mocking how someone speaks or behaves, frequent insults, or actual threats. Even though verbal bullying can occur with both genders, it is most commonly associated with female bullies who tend to be more comfortable with verbal harassment tactics.

*Emotional bullying*

Emotional or relationship bullying involves exploiting personal relationships to hurt other people emotionally. This can be an extremely subtle form of bullying, since it isn't often apparent to people on the outside. For example, someone could bully a spouse by threatening him or her with emotional withdrawal if he or she doesn't behave in a specific way (especially common in abusive relationships when one partner tries to isolate a spouse from family or friends and make them more dependent.) Dominant people in friendships may also use this kind of bullying to intimidate friends with the fear of social isolation if they fail to live up to the expectations the bully has of them.

*Cyberbullying*

With the rise of telecommunications, online social media engines such as Facebook and Twitter have become increasing important as a way of helping friends stay in touch with each other. Unfortunately, it has also spawned a new form of bullying that can be even more devastating and more frequent than any of the other kinds.

Cyberbullying involves the use of technology to harass or intimidate people online, whether in the form of abusive texts or emails, posting revealing photos or videos of people, or spreading false rumors about victims to humiliate them. What makes cyberbullying so effective is that it can be completely anonymous and, as a result, can involve people who have never met in real life and who may be harassing victims for a wide range of reasons.

This means that victims rarely, if ever, have any way of confronting their attackers or forcing them to stop. While most modern police forces have "cybercrime" squads, most cyberbullying falls into a "gray area" that makes it extremely difficult to prosecute, assuming that the bully can be found at all.

People who bully rarely rely on one form of bullying alone (except perhaps for cyberbullying), and most bullying involve a combination of different forms of intimidation, including physical, verbal, and relational.

It can also involve a single bully or an extended group of bullies who "mob" their victims. Whatever form bullying takes, its impact on the victim can leave emotional scars that can last a lifetime.

*How Widespread Is Bullying?*

It's hard to determine just how prevalent bullying is worldwide. Though most research into bullying has focused on high income countries, it can happen anywhere and affect people in all age groups.

Studies of bullying in adolescents have estimated that about twenty to twenty-five percent of all young people report having been bullied at least once though these numbers vary widely.

This ultimately depends on how bullying is defined or whether it is even recognized as bullying in some cultures. In one of the few international studies looking at bullying in adolescents, the overall prevalence rate was around 30 percent, though this fluctuated widely across eighty-three different countries.

Considering how widespread bullying can be, especially among children, it's hardly surprising that the World Health Organization has declared it to be a serious health issue. Still, given that many bullying victims may refuse to tell anyone about what is happening, it often unaddressed and under-reported. As a result, the bullying goes on without anything being done to stop it...or even properly measure it.

Studies in adult survivors of bullying indicate that it can be most severe in people belonging to disadvantaged groups (i.e., racial, religious, or sexual minorities), people with lower education or who come from poorer homes, and people without strong family or community support. As a result, they are usually less able to escape from the bullying and experience chronic trauma which can greatly reinforce the impact that such bullying has in the long run. Not only can this lead to long-term mental health problems, but may result in the bullying victims committing suicide, developing substance abuse and other symptoms.

## *Understanding Childhood Trauma*

While trauma can occur at any age, when we talk about childhood trauma, we are referring to trauma occurring before the age of seventeen. Childhood trauma can take many forms including childhood physical, emotional, or sexual abuse occurring inside the home (by a close family member or caregiver), witnessing domestic violence, or through exposure to a single traumatic event (such as an accidental death or serious injury of someone close to the child).

And then there is bullying which can take place either in school where a child is supposedly safe or even in the home (bullying by a parent or a sibling is distressingly common in many households.)

In one U.S. survey looking at more than 4500 children ranging in age from 0 to 17, more than 60 percent of children had experienced at least one traumatic event in the previous year with almost half experiencing a physical assault. At least one third had experienced two or more direct victimizations with more than 10 percent experiencing five or more.

Research has consistently identified childhood trauma as being the most reliable predictor of lifetime psychiatric problems such as mental illness, vulnerability to PTSD developing later in life, problems forming relationships, poor self-esteem, and long-term feelings of shame and guilt.

And this can apply to all forms of trauma that children and adolescents may experience, including physical, sexual, and emotional trauma.

One all-too-common example, that most people overlook, is the verbal and physical violence that can take place in a household.

Imagine two parents disagreeing in front of a child. While dispute in marriage is nothing strange, many couples escalate a disagreement to exaggerated levels, whether due to their own personal traumas, or due to a lack of understanding about how severe these arguments can be, and how they might affect their child.

We mentioned emotional bullying just previously; now imagine those same tactics being used in an argument between two parents. The child witnesses insults, emotional blackmail, verbal cruelty, seemingly all of a sudden between the two people he loves most in life.

Whose side does he take? Which parent is correct? What are they even fighting about, and why are they *so* angry?

This essentially splits the child in two every time it occurs - they have no context or ability to understand the cause of the argument, the history leading up to it, and especially, whose side to take.

Multiply this by the many times that parents argue and disagree, and you can understand how someone might grow up in an apparently 'normal' family, yet develop traumas that they carry with them into adulthood.

They've been fed a series of experiences, they had no way to understand, and their parents never even knew they were contributing to this future trauma.

While positive childhood experiences can help protect children from the long-term effects of such trauma, that is by no means enough in many cases.

Along with mental health issues, childhood trauma has been linked to a surprising number of physical conditions such as heart disease, stroke, diabetes, substance abuse, and an impaired immune system.

*Can Victims of Bullying Become Bullies Themselves?*

For adolescents in particular, anger is the most common symptom and can lead to problems with emotional control, both as young people and as adults. This includes long-term anger problems and proneness towards violence directed against other people (such as domestic abuse) or themselves in the form of extreme risk-taking behavior. They can also become more isolated and alone due to being unable to form intimate relationships with other people and may even drive others away.

Sadly, this can also mean engaging in bullying behaviors, including cyberbullying, as a way of making themselves feel better or to take the pressure off themselves by helping their bullies find other victims. According to social learning theory, children learn behaviors based on their own experiences or by modeling the behaviors of other people that surround them, especially adults. This means that children exposed to emotionally traumatizing behaviors such as verbal or physical abuse can learn to internalize these behaviors and regard them as normal.

As a result, a "cycle of violence" can develop which they then perpetuate by doing the same to other people in their lives, including their spouses and children.

Along with learning to regard abuse as normal, victims of childhood abuse are also likely to develop long-term personality problems that can make this kind of bullying much easier for them. For example, research has shown that victims of childhood abuse are more likely to develop antisocial and narcissistic personality traits as a way of coping with their trauma. They are also more likely to experience emotional numbing and other dissociative traits that can make it easier to justify how they behave towards others.

Family attitudes or behavior relating to bullying also seems to have a powerful influence on how people respond to childhood abuse. Receiving emotional support from one or both parents can help protect children from developing long-term trauma issues and so can support from friends.

Receiving this kind of support can be crucial in preventing or reducing the kind of emotional problems and help people become more resistant to future bullying.

Earlier in this book, we discussed the difference between posttraumatic stress disorder (PTSD) and chronic posttraumatic stress disorder (C-PTSD) which can certainly apply to people who are bullied for long periods of time with no real relief.

In a recent study, more than 1200 adolescents between the age of twelve and sixteen were assessed using psychometric tests of trauma. Of these adolescents, more than 900 (71.9 percent) reported being exposed to at least one traumatic event during their lifetime with 205 meeting the formal criteria for either PTSD or C-PTSD. For those diagnosed with C-PTSD, bullying proved to be a major factor with a significant impact on quality of life and overall functioning both as adolescents and in later adulthood. C-PTSD adolescents were also more likely to report learning problems in school, problems at home due to conflicts with family, and financial difficulties.

*Is Bullying Changing over Time?*

As cyberbullying becomes more common, what does this mean for other kinds of bullying? The same research that shows cyberbullying becoming much more prevalent also shows that face-to-face (FTF) bullying has remained constant over time.

According to one recent study, while FTF bullying is becoming less common for boys, it is actually increasing for girls. Children who are seen as different, whether they belong to a specific minority or because they have other characteristics that might make them targets are more likely to be subjected to cyberbullying these days though physical, verbal, and emotional bullying are also still happening in many places.

In our ongoing goal to help people recuperate from trauma, there are recurring themes and issues we must address. One of the most challenging social problems that remains prevalent today is Bullying. For many generations, experts have been trying to decipher human behavior in order to address this issue that not only affects one person but the society as a whole.

Bullying is a deliberate and destructive act that is repeatedly and overtly manifested by a bully against another person with the intent to cause psychological, social and physical harm. It affects the person's mental health, breaks his self-esteem and destroys his social relationships.

The gravity of the repercussions can be even more detrimental, traumatic and unconscionable should the person continue to be a bully and a victim.

Although society views the bully as the main predator that should need reform, it is not always the case. Most often, the bully and the victim are at some point sufferers of an erstwhile trauma that could have triggered a drastic change in their behavior—one being aggressive while the other submissive. Both are victims. Both can suffer long-term consequences.

As we navigate the complexities of the modern world, the time-tested wisdom of ancient practices offers a beacon of hope in our quest for holistic healing and self-discovery. In this captivating exploration, we delve into the intricate process of healing the subconscious mind and the significance of integrating ancient wisdom into contemporary therapy.

The subconscious mind operates beneath the threshold of our conscious awareness, harboring a treasure trove of information, experiences, and beliefs that shape our thoughts, emotions, and behaviors. When unresolved trauma or negative beliefs take root in the subconscious, they can manifest as anxiety, depression, addiction, or other mental health challenges. To genuinely heal and grow, we must address the root causes of these issues hidden deep within the subconscious mind.

# 2. THE PATHWAYS TOWARD TRUTH

Many portions of this book will rely on a 'top-down' approach, in that we reach for the core truth behind an issue or challenge in order to both simplify it and find the most logical solution.

To do this, it is important we structure the way in which we search for knowledge. Especially in a world with 'information' overload (and we use quotations purposely), having a framework with which to reach for truth is essential.

As human beings, we all draw from our own experiences, beliefs, philosophies and truths as we shape the reality of our existence.

To some, organized religion has been a source of peace and truth, to others, it's the study of science and the natural world, to others, it's a combination of both - in reality, everyone's path to truth is personal.

In tackling subjects as fundamental as this, it is crucial that I share a bit about Kabbalah, the absolute pillar around which I have framed my research, and my years working with individuals suffering from trauma and the myriad challenges it can bring.

I often draw from and reference Kabbalah as a key basis of the work done by myself and the team in the analysis and healing of trauma. Having studied it for over 35 years and counting, it is absolutely fundamental in my ability to work with individuals through their experiences. Being so important to the topics in this book, it's natural, we want to help understand those who are not familiar with the concept.

Science is, and will always be, about studying and understanding the fundamental elements of the physical world. It has been crucial to our evolution as a species, and a cornerstone of everything that humanity has achieved.

However, when we look at the depth of potential, and the expanse of the subconscious mind, it becomes evident, even to the most secular person, that there exists a world beyond simply the physical.

Purely secular scientific minds may refer to it as energy, religious ones will refer to the soul, and, as is common in today's new age pursuits, it is frequently simply acknowledged that it is one of the unknown elements of the human experience, and is ultimately something we hope to define 'eventually', but can be content knowing it is something out there.

It is these areas where Kabbalah is at an advantage, as the Kabbalistic study of truth has been rooted in both the physical and spiritual world from the beginning of recorded history. It is equally comfortable discussing astronomy and parallel realities, as it is discussing consciousness and spiritual awareness.

And as we move into greater and greater understanding of how trauma is connected to our psyche and the world beyond ourselves - Kabbalah has been an indispensable tool for both the work described herein, and the understanding of how the physiological processes of the body relate to the energy that powers our very essence as people.

## *Understanding the energy within us*

While much of this book will talk about the subconscious, how its depth and capability for storing memories is crucial to who we are as individuals, and how we relate to the larger universe around us; however, there are a few key elements of our conscious mind that we must discuss in order to fully appreciate what comes next.

If we hope to understand trauma, we must also understand what trauma can prevent us from experiencing, or even more accurately, what pieces of the universal experience it may limit us from accessing.

Have you ever felt deeply connected to someone? A family member, a lover, or even someone you'd just met.

Likely, that's a feeling you know well; the sensation of trust, positivity, and altruism that is triggered in those moments of happiness around others.

Some of us are fortunate enough to experience this on a regular basis, and for those of us who have experienced trauma, it can often feel like those sensations are a distant memory.

For this reason, a part of the scope of this book will be to investigate and highlight the ways in which we can access this positive energy, and free ourselves from the many obstacles that trauma can put in our path, to block us from it.

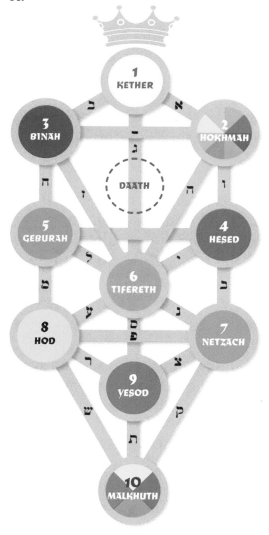

In Kabbalah, this concept is called Chesed. Without completely losing my audience by doing a deep-dive, I'd like to take a few moments to describe Chesed in the way it's revealed to us through Kabbalah, as one of the 10 key channels of the divine, or of the creative life force.

In its simplest form, Chesed or Hesed (pronounced heh-sed) refers to, essentially, the concept of "loving kindness" - it is the sum result of altruism, gratitude, generosity, charity and sharing, without any expectation of getting anything in return.

And it's one of the most tangible forces that drive our existence.

Chesed refers not only to the concept that we can and should consciously pursue these positive connections, but the truth that we can't really live without them.

When I say this, I don't mean that it's a 'nice to have' - I mean that it's a fundamental force of the universe, and a driving force behind human behavior and motivations.

For our Isaac Newton fans, we can refer to the first law of thermodynamics: Energy can be neither created nor destroyed, only altered in form.

We can choose to channel energy around positivity...or we can do the opposite. The world can and does send anything our way: traumas, challenges, joy and suffering. Not a single one of us is immune to the highs and lows of life, and we all have our crosses to bear. What we can do, in fact what we *must* do, is choose how we respond, and how we pass that energy along and using it in the correct way.

Moving right along to the second law of thermodynamics, we know that every action has an equal and opposite reaction.

Put another way, if I push someone, I either dig my heels in or I'm going to feel a momentum and take a step back, right? Practitioners of Judo know this extremely well - the momentum of their opponent becomes the power of the defender.

It is not a question of generating the energy or momentum, but simply channeling and reversing it to achieve the goal of defense.

Now, imagine that every act of kindness has the same effect. Every kind word, every peaceful gesture, every hug, every gift, and every helping hand charges us back with an equal amount of positive energy.

There's a reason we truly feel good when we're being kind. And it's not by accident - it's because the universe is designed that way.

It's evident: when we see that a child is in trouble, our instincts immediately kick in and we spring into action before we can even think. That's because the altruism center of the brain is considered a "deep brain structure," part of the primitive brain, and simply a fundamental part of the physiology of our mind.

Humans are social animals, so it makes perfect sense that we're hardwired to care. In our complex modern society, the benefits of sharing and cooperation can be witnessed every day, but more and more, through chemical and neuroscientific research, we now understand that both the giver and receiver benefit from the relationship, in tangible physical ways.

There are plenty of supporting bits of research we can look at to show the effects between kindness and positive reactions in the brain.

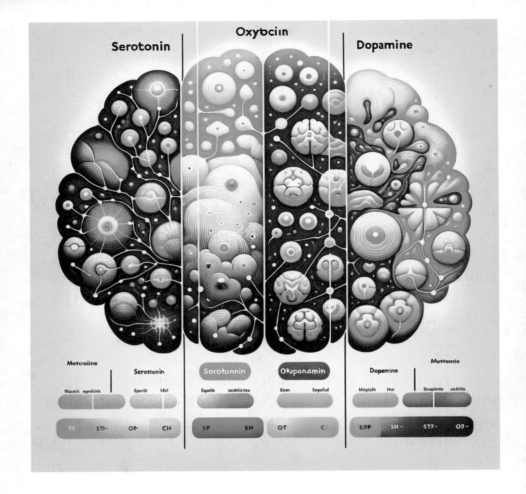

*Kindness is chemical*

From a physiological level, there is a wealth of info uncovering the truth that releases hormones that contribute to your mood and overall well-being. The practice is so effective it's being formally incorporated into some types of psychotherapy.

"We all seek a path to happiness," says Dr. Waguih William IsHak, a professor of psychiatry at Cedars-Sinai. "Practicing kindness toward others is one we know works."

According to Cedars-Sinai, the bulk of research supporting this concept of kindness, and how it physically improves our state of being, has been focused on what is commonly called "the love hormone."

This is none other than oxytocin. Most research on the science behind why kindness makes us feel better has centered around oxytocin. It's often called "the love hormone" and with good reason.

It's intrinsic in the process of forming social bonds and establishing trust with other people. It's also a key component of physical intimacy, getting released during sex, cuddling, and makes up a crucial part of helping us be more generous and friendlier. It even lowers our blood pressure.

But it's not just oxytocin that gets a boost from kindness.

Studies have also shown that random acts of kindness can release dopamine, which differs from oxytocin in that, while also a euphoric sensation, is tied to feelings of reward, accomplishment, and motivation. It's the dominant chemical triggered, as many will have learned in the digital age, through activities like video games, their bleeps and bloops when achieving something, and even likes and notifications on social media, for better or worse.

Dopamine is connected to motivation and arousal.

It also is released with the moment of accomplishment we experience when giving a helping hand to someone. This is often referred to in psychological circles as "helper's high".

Regardless of the source, it's a chemical messenger in the brain that can give us immediate feelings of euphoria, and a key part of our general emotional wellbeing, one reason why it's increasingly important to stimulate this hormone through human interactions rather than the digital stimuli that have often co-opted this hormone.

There is one more hormone that is considered part of the 'Happiness Trifecta', and we're lucky that it is also greatly stimulated through kindness to others.s

Serotonin, as opposed to dopamine, however, is associated with general sensations of happiness, calmness, and has a direct relation to one's overall mood.

It's also connected to sleep, digestion, memory, learning, and appetite.

While the brain is remarkably complex, the neurochemical drivers of happiness are quite easy to identify. Dopamine, serotonin, and oxytocin are the chemical keys to happiness. Therefore, any activity that increases the production of these neurochemicals will cause a boost in mood. It's really that simple.

When these chemicals flow, a number of things happen at once. Blood pressure decreases, bonding increases, social fears are reduced and trust and empathy are enhanced, to name a few. Some of the effects go much farther than simply mood.

Oxytocin, for instance, is also an anti-inflammatory and reduces pain and enhances wound healing.

Healing? Well, yes.

## Chesed and Healing

As a Rabbi, as I conduct my research, I frequently discover that scientific phenomena that I come across through studies, are already reflected in key passages in the Torah.

This is one of my favorite elements of studying both scripture and science simultaneously, the joy of understanding that both are referencing universal truths.

There is one particular event I can reference about Abraham, in the book of Genesis, that reflects this concept neatly.

At this point in the scripture, Abraham is already known as a symbol of altruism and generosity in the community and is already recognized as the leader of the known world.

In this anecdote, however, we find Abraham sitting outside the front of his tent and home, during a very historic moment.

You see, two days prior, he has become the first man to be circumcised as part of the new covenant with the creator, and needless to say, there is a lot of pain involved.

Rather than being bedridden and recuperating, however, he is sitting outside, in excruciating pain no less, with the anticipation of being able to receive someone, anyone, for hospitality.

As luck would have it, three wanderers appeared, and he immediately rushed to them, offering them water, food, and rest.

In this moment, Abraham, who is suffering great physical pain, is still more concerned with helping others than with tending to his own discomfort.

How can a man in such pain even think about attending to others, doing hospitality and serving people during a time of recuperation? It doesn't appear logical.

Well, for a man so accustomed to integrating Chesed in every moment of his life, being forced to stop, to put his generosity on pause, increased his pain, rather than eased it.

As a Rabbi, I naturally go deeper into the text and spend what feels like an eternity trying to interpret the core truth behind these passages. When a scientific study helps me see something in a new light, it's often a stunning revelation.

With all of the above considered, I can clearly see that Abraham, in this moment, is an example to us, a guiding light giving us only a glimpse of what is possible by submitting more of ourselves to altruism every day.

Abraham, as with all of us to this very day, benefits greatly from his continued commitment to Chesed, even though self-interest was in no way the purpose of his gesture.

Helping others through their own discomfort in the desert was second nature to him, but in return, the universe passes that energy right back to him, and helps speed his recuperation, not hinder it.

Through the scientific studies described above regarding oxytocin, dopamine, and serotonin, we find that very answer, and see the core truth contained in these passages in the Torah. And to be clear, this has nothing to do with attempting to educate readers on bible or theology; rather, it is about illustrating not only a great example, but showing this concept is so ancient and understood by mankind throughout the ages, that it should be considered a fundamental principle to everything else we will talk about, especially our method on how we heal individuals from trauma.

Brought back to our contemporary lifestyle, if giving often, and being generous, allows us to secrete all the positive brain chemicals at once, we owe it to ourselves to give as often as possible.

## So How do we Do This?

Helping others can take on many forms. Small repeated boosts of the Happiness Trifecta will produce the most benefit so it's importance to find ways to give and to give often.

Opening a door for someone, letting someone in on the highway, donating money or time, helping a tourist find their way around, or listening to someone or giving advice are all wonderful ways to stay connected to the spirit of regular giving. Every time we take a moment to step outside of ourselves long enough to make a positive effect in someone else's life, something wonderful happens: our team of three neurochemicals is boosted!

Some specific and instinctual aspects of our psyche are triggered as well, through this process.

Empathy: The brain is structured with elements focused specifically on helping you see things from someone else's perspective. When we take the time to step into another person's shoes, and ideally even help them get what they need in a given moment, we give these areas a workout, strengthening their capabilities.

Mirror Neurons: Referencing, once again, the social aspects of being a human, our instincts are designed to help us connect. Mixed in with the other benefits of altruism is this unmistakable effect: when we see someone smile at us, our brain really wants us to smile too. It's all because, when you smile at someone, you trigger their mirror neurons. Both the giver and the receiver, then, can directly impact the other's brain in a positive way.

In short, large or small, every act of giving and kindness pays off, and the more regular, the better. 'Giving' doesn't refer to actual gifts or monetary donations, either. Giving time, giving energy, and giving moments all count. Is there a cause you support? A friend that needs a hand? A stranger that could use a random act of kindness?

Small acts of giving, especially when integrated into daily life, are a wildly effective way to bring happiness to yourself and others. Even just smiling at someone is an act of giving and will brighten both of your days. You can give one away multiple times a day at no cost, and in the process boost your mood and your health.

Don't limit yourself to the usual - be creative with new ways to help. The next time you're checking out at the supermarket, try something out of the ordinary: give a compliment, add a lighthearted comment, or outright give an unexpected well-wish like "I hope everyone is nice to you today!" instead of a standard "thanks" and you're almost guaranteed to get a smile. "Great to see you!" and "You did a good job on that project!" don't cost you anything, yet everyone gains. Combine expressions of kindness like this with a smile and you'll boost your investment and your return.

Think about the news, and the amount of negativity we are exposed to through that medium - which innocent people died today? What injustices did we witness? Which aspect of society is failing us? These are simply questions we are bombarded with day in and day out. In a world where we often spend more hours of the day looking at our phones or computers than actually interacting with other people, imagine the effect a little bit of positivity can have.

As we've seen, people crave that smile, they yearn for that kind word, and are desperate for more moments with loved ones, whether they know it or not. This makes it so powerful when a person receives positivity when they least expect it, at work, while shopping, while driving, or simply while standing in line. Those who are able to give that shot of positivity stand out, and create a result that can instinctively cause others lives to change, even if only a little at a time.

Great things can have small beginnings, and a practiced and consistent approach to altruism, and the rewards it can provide to others and yourself can lead you to even larger outpourings of generosity you may not yet have imagined.

In a personal case, I've been able to feel the deep benefits of the generosity mindset, and it has become ingrained in my habits. For example, when I observe Shabbat, many times I have 30 people with me. People ask me "how do you not go crazy?" The fact is, I simply cannot go without it, I have to do Chesed, it's my own source of therapy.

So give, give often, and bask in the mental and physical effects of your actions.

No matter how it's measured or tracked, the evidence stands up for itself, whether it's in a study or in the way you feel when rushing up to someone after they dropped their wallet.

But the conscious elements of kindness are only a minuscule fraction of the story. As we delve into the following section on the power of the subconscious, I want you to remember that everything we do and feel in our waking mind is reflected a thousand-fold within the infinite depths of our subconscious.

And when we heal from the factors blocking our true ability to participate in Chesed, to be deeply connected to the vibrations of altruism and positivity that surround us, it is then that we can truly begin to engage with one of the most powerful forces that we as living creatures, and every other soul in the universe is given access to. And this all has to do with our method for healing trauma, as we will show in the upcoming chapter.

So, not only does Chesed heal, but it is also the reward for healing. It is with this understanding that we move forward into discussing our greatest partner for helping us stay a vital part of this cycle: our own subconscious.

By understanding the true power of the subconscious mind, and its influence over us, we will get one step closer to showing the methods we've discovered to *definitively* heal from trauma.

# 3. THE ROAD TO THERAPY THROUGH UNDERSTANDING OF THE SUBCONSCIOUS

The human body sends 11 million bits per second to the brain for processing, yet the conscious mind seems to be able to process only 50 bits per second.

That's like processing over 100GB of data a day.

Put another way, if your body is a company, and your conscious mind is one employee, stimulate the power of the subconscious, and it's like hiring 220,000 more employees.

Of all the things we experience, feel, process, remember and forget, the fact is, what we consciously are aware of is but a fraction. Around 1 in 220,000 to be precise...

Not only is the subconscious managing which bits of info, emotion, and perception make it through the filter into our conscious reality, it's managing thousands of physical processes we take for granted in every waking moment. To research the subconscious, then, is to research the whole human.

According to Kabbalah, that very power of our mind allows us to be connected to entire universes of information and energy.

A key tenet of our research, and of this book, is that it is our subconscious not only stores the records of all our experiences (and of course, our traumas), but continues to affect us during every moment of our lives.

When it comes to trauma, the subconscious has a very unique relationship with these past experiences.

You see, trauma has some very curious attributes.

One critical one, is that there seems to be compelling reasons why someone wouldn't want to forget it but also why they wouldn't want to remember it either. It's a bit like a treasured possession that you keep in the attic. It has great value, and you can't let it go, but it's kept out of sight.

To learn more about how deep memory can affect our waking lives, we can look to the animal kingdom.

Some recent research with zebrafish suggests that at least in these relatively simple organisms, procedural memory related to how an organism learns to do something, changes with increasing training.

In these studies, when these fish were re-trained, two key neurological things happened almost simultaneously.

As they learned new skills, it appeared that older memories were eliminated and replaced by new ones. This research was the first to demonstrate neurological activity of wiping out old memories and simultaneously replacing them with new ones.

This makes perfect sense. Why would you need to use up valuable Neurological RAM with outdated information - info that could also be a detriment to the development of new and better skills?

Do you have an app that cleans up your computer memory? You know what I mean, the app that removes copies of files and apps you no longer use, freeing up memory for newer, more relevant and important stuff. It makes perfect sense that the conscious brain, desperate for storage space, would have the same mechanism.

So far, this all makes sense. So, why aren't nasty memories of traumatic events similarly removed?

The need for storage space is critical and perhaps only superseded by one other priority – survival.

Here's an example many can resonate with - when we suffer a serious accident - why do we pass out? In fact, this is one of the brilliant ways our body helps us survive.

When we've suffered heavy physical trauma, the body knows that we may be wounded and bleeding - that's bad, and it requires quick thinking on the part of our body to keep us safe.

Because keeping the blood pumping slowly is so crucial to avoid blood loss, we often pass out. Ok, but why? Imagine being awake and seeing a gaping wound in your body - what would happen? You'd panic, right? Or at minimum have an increase in anxiety. That means a faster heart rate, and quicker blood loss.

To prevent this, the body simply removes the conscious mind from the equation. You pass out, and the subconscious takes over to do what is necessary to survive.

Surviving from emotional trauma is very similar.

The mind will always do what is most efficient for survival in the moment, and that means filtering and processing memories quickly.

If a memory is critical for survival, it needs to be maintained, no matter how old it is.

We can only speculate exactly how such memories are preserved but it absolutely has to do with the level of emotion that accompanies the original experience.

And encounters that involve survival are likely to be emotionally volatile. Evidence suggests that a specific neurotransmitter, norepinephrine, is implicated in this process.

Trauma researcher Bessel van der Kolk wrote in a 2002 paper:

"While response to stress evokes mechanisms that lead to self-conservation and resource re-allocation, trauma involves a unique combination of hyperarousal, learned conditioning and shattered meaning propositions."

Let's translate this observation into regular language. What the research quote is communicating is that, as opposed to simple everyday stress, true trauma goes beyond that response, and laboratory research proves to us that it activates reactions that go into our very core.

One of the challenges with traumatic memories is that, because they are so loaded with emotion and uncomfortable hyperarousal, they are encoded into the entire organism of the person.

As a result, and because of the discomfort we feel when we try to consciously think about our trauma, it is most often reflected as bodily sensations.

These are often, but not limited to, extreme arousal and anxiety; they could include physical pain in different parts of the body or other apparently mysterious and uncomfortable or stressful feelings.

There is the presence of highly specific sensations but often a confusion about the specifics that can't be easily verbalized, or talked about at all.

Interestingly, these sensations are often remembered with reliable accuracy over time. However, the interpretation of what they mean and the circumstances around the original experience can change as people try to verbalize their meaning. This is especially true of people who were traumatized as children.

As children, they were likely to have had difficulty articulating their experiences to themselves making the meaning difficult to extract and certainly communicate to others. They were also likely to have engaged in dissociation, making full access to their traumatic experiences and feelings almost impossible and by definition, disjointed and confusing.

Subsequently, this confusion does make traumatized individuals vulnerable to the suggestions of others, or even environmental factors, as they struggle to piece together the meaning of heightened but disconnected sensations.

As these sensations remain trapped in the mind and body, they can be triggered by any associated cue, which is not intrinsically emotional but can stimulate traumatic sensations.

For example, someone who was brutally attacked in a park can have traumatic sensations elicited by *any* of the cues that were present, like a particular bush, flower or even the sight of a park bench. Such seemingly innocent triggers, can all of a sudden bring up very unpleasant associations and sensations. And such sensations can and will activate the "fight or flight" system in the same way that an active "fight or flight system" can elicit traumatic memories.

They are always connected. And this is a key to understanding how to disconnect them, and move a person forward from that stuck experience.

Indeed, while we know it from experience talking to thousands of people, the physical research shows it just the same. Trauma is related to significant brain changes including the reduction in the size of the hippocampus, and abnormal development in the amygdala and other associated regions where emotions are processed.

What we feel emotionally is reflected in our actual brain science.

As the science explains:

"In many instances, traumatized individuals report a combination of both extreme vividness, or a total resistance to the imagery. While people seem to easily assimilate familiar and expectable experiences and while memories of ordinary events disintegrate in clarity over time, some aspects of traumatic events appear to get fixed in the mind, unaltered by the passage of time or by the intervention of subsequent experience. For example, in our own studies on posttraumatic nightmares, subjects claimed that they saw the same traumatic scenes over and over again without modification over a 15-year period."

Put another way, the subconscious, having a crystal clear record of the traumatic experience, can serve up certain images to our conscious mind with such clarity, yet without the full necessary context with which to understand them.

As we mention in the park example above, any stimulus, seemingly innocent, might trigger one of these deep memories. These images are often pieces of the event, presented as isolated echoes. Their effect, however, can be anything but innocent, causing a sharp survival reaction in the person. What is perceived as a nightmare, in essence, is truly a brief glimpse at the truth, if only we could understand that. This fact, is yet another element of the treatments we have developed that have shown to be able to completely release the buried traumatic memories.

## Why does trauma stick around the way it does?

Indeed, trauma leaves a footprint. And it is this very footprint that causes a person to remain overwhelmed by it. If this footprint is not resolved, it is essentially a force continuing to press down on the person's existence. While a traumatic event in the past may have been relatively short, the trauma, and its effects are 'long', like the roots of a tree, expanding ever further into the soil of the subconscious. And these roots connect between our conscious, our physical reaction, and our emotions.

Over a hundred years ago, the famous memory researcher Pierre Janet wrote…

"Forgetting the event which precipitated the emotion…has frequently been found to accompany intense emotional experiences in the form of continuous and retrograde amnesia… They are an exaggerated form of a general disturbance of memory which is characteristic of all emotions".

Put another way, when people are very emotional, they cannot create a non-emotional narrative about what they are feeling. They simply can't create a version of the event that is removed from these powerful emotions.

This keeps these events removed from the logical mind, and prevents a meaningful integration of such events in their personal story, and thus continues to keep them separated from consciousness.

Without having a meaningful and personal narrative about these traumatic sensations, they remain isolated horrors that cannot be removed.

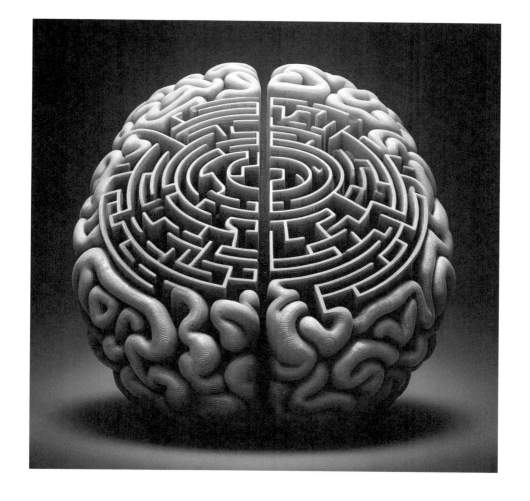

Until these sensations can be processed, they remain as parts of the sensory components of an unclear experience. They exist as images, smells, touch, physical sensations that cannot be understood or examined because they can't be verbalized in the same way we do every other element of our personas.

What research shows is that, during activation of the traumatic memory, the brain thinks it is actually *living* its experience. Think about it, imagine your body is convincing you that you're literally reliving your life's most horrible experience. You feel, see, or hear the sensory elements of the traumatic experience.

You might be physiologically impaired from being able to properly understand this experience and express it in language while you are remembering it.

You might suffer from speechless terror, literally `out of touch with your feelings'.

As a result, the body may respond as if it is being traumatized again, secreting all the various neurohormones that are mobilized on these occasions.

The victim cannot `own' what is happening, and thus cannot take steps to do anything about it.

The sensations of trauma, therefore, exist in the mind-body, and are difficult to access in a meaningful way. The mind is not verbal in itself, and trying to articulate these physical sensations is a major challenge, requiring an overwhelmed consciousness to turn these disparate feelings into a meaningful story.

That is one reason why it is often easier for others, rather than the traumatized person, to create a narrative about those haunting past events.

*So what can the subconscious mind cause us to do?*

As we outline the method of healing, we now move into further analysis and evidence of how our inner mind can shape and alter our behaviors.

Luckily, there are many references and studies we can turn to for simple proof. Here's an example from a Yale study about how the subconscious mind can, in a way, 'take the driver's seat' of our perceptions and actions without us even knowing it consciously.

Before we describe it, it's important to understand why this is a clear example. What is shows it that our behaviors can (and are) altered every day by information that our conscious mind simply isn't aware of.

In the experiment, psychologists at Yale altered people's judgments of a stranger by handing them a cup of coffee.

The study participants, college students, had no idea that their social instincts were being deliberately manipulated.

On the way to the laboratory, they had bumped into a laboratory assistant, who was holding textbooks, a clipboard, papers and a cup of hot or iced coffee — and asked for a hand with the cup.

That was all it took: The students who held a cup of iced coffee rated a hypothetical person they later read about as being much colder, less social and more selfish than did their fellow students, who had momentarily held a cup of hot coffee.

Now imagine, that simple, unemotional cup of coffee, whose temperature affected only one small impression later in the day, was the persistent drumming of massive emotions from past trauma? What day to day decisions might that affect?

Studies like this one about the coffee, as improbable as they seem, have poured forth in psychological research over the last few years. Each one gives a great example of the types of choices people make based on what's hidden within.

For example, other studies have found that people tidy up more thoroughly when there's a faint tang of cleaning liquid that has been placed in the air; they become more competitive if there's a briefcase placed in sight, or more cooperative if they glimpse words like "dependable" and "support" — all without being aware of the change, or what prompted it.

Psychologists say that "priming" people in this way is not some form of hypnotism, or even subliminal seduction; rather, it's a demonstration of how everyday sights, smells and sounds can selectively activate goals or motives that people already have.


More fundamentally, the new studies reveal a subconscious brain that is far more active, purposeful and independent than previously known. Goals, whether to eat, mate or devour an iced latte, are like neural software programs that can only be run one at a time, and the unconscious is perfectly capable of running the program it chooses.

The give and take between these unconscious choices and our rational, conscious aims can help explain some of the more mystifying realities of behavior, like how we can be generous one moment and petty the next, or act rudely at a dinner party when convinced we are the very picture of charm.

How has society viewed the subconscious's influence?

We're at a point in history where people are beginning to finally understand the power of tools like ibogaine which can be used, only by someone with the right experience and knowledge to properly administer it*, to help release a person from the remaining effects of their own traumatic experiences. But awareness of the subconscious's importance has been down a long road, even recently!

Kids growing up in the 80's and 90s may remember a brief moral panic in the media about the worry about subliminal messaging; concerns over everything from advertising, to the idea of satanic messaging hidden in rock albums.

The idea of subliminal influence has a mixed reputation among scientists because of a history of advertising hype and apparent fraud. But this skepticism can all be traced back to one root event.

In 1957, an ad man named James Vicary claimed to have increased sales of Coca-Cola and popcorn at a movie theater in Fort Lee, N.J., by secretly flashing the words "Eat popcorn" and "Drink Coke" during the film, too quickly to be consciously noticed. But advertisers and regulators doubted his story from the beginning, and in a 1962 interview, Mr. Vicary acknowledged that he had inflated his findings to gain attention for his business.

Later studies of products promising subliminal improvement, for things like memory and self-esteem, found no effect. The skepticism that arose from this advertising example (which also caused some damage to Coke's reputation during the scandal) may have set back the belief and research about the subconscious's role for decades, as it was politicized by everyone from cultural analysts to anti-censorship activists.

But we've come a long way since then. In the decades since, most in the field now agree that proof of the subconscious's role is far too strong.

Make no mistake, while no significant studies have emerged showing that split-second subliminal cues can make a *long-term* difference in a test audience, change the length of these cues to something more perceptible, and the story changes.

When we talk about visual and emotional triggers, the evidence can be overwhelming on how the subconscious can be in the driver's seat of our reactions and behaviors, so long as the stimulus can be adequately perceived, even if not consciously acknowledged.

Let's look at yet another an example from a noted study.

In a 2004 experiment, psychologists at Stanford University and now at the University of Waterloo, had students take part in a one-on-one investment game with another, unseen player.

Students were separated into two rooms, where they could not see each other.

Half the students played while sitting at a large table, at the other end of which was a briefcase and a black leather portfolio. The other students played in an identical room, but with a simple backpack on the table instead.

What do you think was the effect?

Interestingly, the students with the briefcase in their room were notably stingier and more careful with their money, vs the backpack students.

The mere presence of the briefcase, noticed but not necessarily registered within the conscious, generated business-related associations and expectations, leading the brain to run the most appropriate program, which was to compete.

The students themselves had no sense of whether they had acted selfishly or generously.

In another experiment, published in 2005, Dutch psychologists asked undergraduate students to sit in a cubicle and fill out a questionnaire.

Hidden in the room was a bucket of water with a splash of citrus-scented cleaning fluid, giving off a faint odor.

After finishing the questionnaire, the young men and women had a snack, a crumbly biscuit provided by laboratory staff members.

The researchers secretly filmed the snack time, and discovered some interesting results. The students who had taken the questionnaire in the room with the lemon scent cleared away crumbs three times more often than a comparison group who had taken the same questionnaire in a room with no cleaning scent.

This is a perfect example of a relatively large difference in behavior, even if it might be seem insignificant, but one driven completely by the subconscious mind.

Now, these are clearly innocuous stimuli, where the emotional stakes are extremely low. So just imagine the effect of the deeply emotional stimuli trauma survivors face every day?

## The Circuits in the Brain

Have you ever gone out to run an errand, like say, going to pick up the drycleaning, but then come back with wine and cigarettes, but without your clean pants? We've all experienced these real world unconscious 'blips'.

The brain appears to use the very same neural circuits to execute an unconscious act as it does a conscious one. In a study that appeared in the journal Science in 2007, a team of English and French neuroscientists performed brain imaging on 18 men and women who were playing a computer game for money.

The players held a handgrip and were told that the tighter they squeezed when an image of money flashed on the screen, the more of the loot they could keep.

As expected, the players squeezed harder when the image of a British pound flashed by than when the image of a penny did — regardless of whether they consciously perceived the pictures, many of which flew by subliminally. But the circuits activated in their brains were similar as well: an area called the ventral pallidum was particularly active whenever the participants responded.

"This area is located in what used to be called the reptilian brain, well below the conscious areas of the brain," said the study's senior author, Chris Frith, a professor in neuropsychology at University College London who wrote the book "Making Up The Mind: How the Brain Creates our Mental World."

The results suggest a "bottom-up" decision-making process, in which the ventral pallidum is part of a circuit that first weighs the reward and decides, then interacts with the higher-level, conscious regions later, if at all.

Scientists have spent years trying to pinpoint the exact neural regions that support conscious awareness, so far in vain. But there's little doubt it involves the prefrontal cortex, the thin outer layer of brain tissue behind the forehead, and experiments like this one show that it can be one of the last neural areas to know when a decision is made.

This bottom-up order makes sense from an evolutionary perspective. The subcortical areas of the brain evolved first and would have had to help individuals fight, flee and scavenge well before conscious, distinctly human layers were added later in evolutionary history.

## What Are the Symptoms of Trauma?

So we've seen how trauma is clearly a powerful force, and can alter our behaviors, but what *can* it actually cause us to feel….and do?

While not everyone exposed to a traumatic event, whether directly or indirectly, is going to develop mental health problems, survivors of trauma often develop emotional issues as a result.

They can include:

*Shock or denial about what they experienced*

People experiencing a traumatic event are often left in a state of shock over what has happened. They can also find themselves having difficulty believing that what they are experiencing is real. In the aftermath of the events of September 11, 2001, many survivors told reporters afterward that they felt as if "they were in a movie": since what they were experiencing was so far outside their regular lives.

This sense of unreality is known as dissociation and, for many people experiencing severe trauma, can leave them completely unable to function, at least for a little while.

How long this sense of shock continues usually varies depending on each individual's own life experiences as well as whether past mental health problems or previous trauma makes them more vulnerable. First responders trying to help people in shock often need to reassure them and, if necessary, force them to get to safety if they are still in danger.

*Guilt or shame over failing to act*

Even after the initial shock and denial subsides, people experiencing trauma may feel guilty over not doing more to help or by getting help from first responders that might have gone to others they feel needed help more.

There is also survivor guilt to contend with, especially when someone is feeling ashamed over being relatively unharmed when other people are severely injured or killed.

This is particularly common after natural or man-made disasters as well as with domestic abuse such as when children feel guilty over their mother or other family member bearing most of the actual abuse while they are left relatively unharmed. Such guilt and shame tend to last for months or years even when other trauma symptoms subside. They hold themselves guilty.

*Anger, irritability, and mood swings as they come to terms with what happened*

For people experiencing trauma, coming to terms with the complex mix of emotions that can come with it can be extremely challenging.

Along with the guilt and shame we've already discussed, they can feel extreme anger, i.e., "how could this happen to me?." This anger can also be directed against the cause of whatever traumatic event brings on the trauma as well as against first responders, health professionals, and relief agencies trying to provide help. Survivors can be angry because they aren't getting enough help, or because of having to deal with bureaucracies, or because people trying to help can't possibly know how they feel.

They might also find themselves lashing out at friends and family who may not be as sympathetic or helpful as they think they deserve. This can often damage their relationship with them and make their recovery more difficult as a result.

Also, since trauma sufferers often find their thoughts racing due to inability to control their emotions, they are also prone to mood swings while processing through their experiences.

*Feelings of sadness or hopelessness*

Not surprisingly, many trauma sufferers are also prone to symptoms of depression such as sadness, loss of energy, difficulty with eating, sleep problems, agitation, and social isolation to name just a few. They may also develop a sense of hopelessness over the belief that "nothing can get better" and that they can never return to their former lives. In a real sense, this is a form of grief over the loss of security brought on by their trauma and the sense that they can never be happy again.

*Mental confusion*

Given the different emotions brought on by trauma, many trauma sufferers often experience mental confusion affecting their ability to think as well as memory and concentration. This is often aggravated by other problems such as poor sleep, nightmares, being preoccupied with memories of the trauma that often blocks other cognitive functions. As a result, people experiencing severe trauma may often feel as if they are going around "in a daze" and unable to focus on tasks related to work or school. Again, this often varies from person to person and can persist for months or years after the trauma first occurs.

## How Does Trauma Unfold As We Grow?

In the case of childhood trauma, one of the more important psychological issues comes into play; How influential are childhood experiences, including trauma, on subsequent development?

There are some who believe that the role one plays in one's family becomes the dominant way of socializing across potentially all relationships. For example, if you are the odd one out in your family, will you take that role into future relationships? After all, that dominant role will likely shape how you view yourself, how you think others view you, and the ways of interacting. Such an idea has an intrinsic rationality but not much independent research. However, there is a major psychological theory that does have substantial research and consideration.

In the 1950s John Bowlby developed Attachment Theory. His notion was that experiences in various stages of development – infancy, childhood, teenage years – had a major impact on subsequent social interaction, self-perception, functioning and mental health.

Attachment Theory suggests that in the first few months of life, the child's relationship with its foremost caregiver – typically the mother – is critical in the development of a sense of safety and control. As the infant matures, this relationship continues to influence his or her sense of safety but in ways that are now commensurate with the age-related skills.

Based on this theory Bowlby suggested different types of attachment dependent on the child's experience.

## Secure Attachment

Secure attachment is the ideal state, when the child explores freely in the presence of the caregiver, interacts with strangers, and might get somewhat anxious when the prime caregiver leaves them, and is happy to see them return.

Securely attached children are best able to explore when they have the knowledge of a secure base (their caregiver) to return to in times of need. When assistance is given, this bolsters the sense of security and also, assuming the parent's assistance is helpful, educates the child on how to cope with the same problem in the future. Therefore, secure attachment can be seen as the most adaptive attachment style.

Evidence (e.g. Aronoff, 2012) shows that such secure attachment is common when parents are loving and responsive to their children in infancy and childhood.

## Anxious-Ambivalent

An anxious ambivalent child doesn't typically explore freely even when the caregiver is present, is wary of strangers and panics, often by crying or screaming, when the caregiver leaves and shows ambivalence when the caregiver returns. Such displays of insecurity and/or frustration and even anger are seen as a way of trying to gain the caregiver's attention when it can't be guaranteed.

The research shows that "resistant behavior is particularly conspicuous. The mixture of seeking and yet resisting contact and interaction has an unmistakably angry quality and indeed an angry tone may characterize behavior in the pre-separation episodes."

McCarthy and Taylor (1999) found that children in abusive relationships would more likely develop this ambivalent-anxious attachment style and more likely to have difficulty maintaining intimate relationships in adulthood.

## Anxious-avoidant and dismissive-avoidant attachment

This attachment style is characterized by avoidance, with the child ignoring the caregiver.

Per Ainsworth et al., (1978) this style is characterized by "conspicuous avoidance of the mother in the reunion episodes which is likely to consist of ignoring her altogether, although there may be some pointed looking away, turning away, or moving away. If there is a greeting when the mother enters, it tends to be a mere look or a smile. Either the baby does not approach his mother upon reunion, or they approach in "abortive" fashions with the baby going past the mother, or it tends to only occur after much coaxing. If picked up, the baby shows little or no contact-maintaining behavior; he tends not to cuddle in; he looks away and he may squirm to get down."

It has been reasonably postulated that the child's detachment is a result of not wanting to be continually rejected. It learns that seeking attachment or even engagement is a losing proposition and thus learns to avoid such disappointment by not seeking it.

## Disorganized/Disoriented

When the infant's behavior seems uncoordinated and variable in the search for caregiver love, it is considered 'disorganized' and symptomatic of anxiety. Such a disorganized/disoriented approach is characterized by anxiety; contradictory actions, misdirected movements and even dissociation.

Studies show that others who were traumatized around the birth of the infant and had become depressed, were more likely to have children with this disorganized/disoriented detachment style. Which raises the question of the relationship between trauma and attachment style, and vice-versa.

The relationship is likely complex. For example, Solomon and George (2006) found that the mother's unresolved loss was more likely to be associated with her infant's disorganized attachment when the mother had also been subject to unresolved trauma prior to the loss.

In the case of secure attachment, one would presume that such an adaptive style is not associated with early trauma, and that should traumatic events subsequently be encountered the person will be most capable of managing it.

The anxious-ambivalent style may be associated with various forms of caregiver abuse.

The anxious avoidant and dismissive avoidant styles could also be indicative of caregiver abuse. However, such an attachment style if maintained, might also contribute to victims of abuse not telling others about their abuse for fear of not being taken seriously or with compassion. The experience of the anxious avoidant child is one of being dismissed constantly.

The Disorganized and Disoriented attachment style also lends itself to potential abuse and again a reluctance to tell anyone about it for fear of not just disbelief, but even worse, lack of compassion and concern.

Attachment Theory does make it very clear that abuse by a caregiver is likely to have a dramatic impact that will affect the development of the social and emotional self for years, if not longer, if left untreated.

In our experience over 15 years in treating trauma, we have seen variations on these types of childhood developments, and yet the paths to healing from them are often surprisingly similar. Since trauma is at the root of all of these, the way to process the trauma remains unchanged. We will outline this process in the coming chapter.

## How Trauma Leads to Bad Habits

The impact of trauma on brain chemistry is one of the predominant forces that can shape a person's life and, subsequently, their behaviors. These changes alter the way an individual perceives and responds to the world around them.

When a person experiences trauma, the brain's stress response system is activated, leading to the release of stress hormones such as cortisol and adrenaline. In some cases, this response can become dysregulated, leading to ongoing hyperarousal and vigilance, even in situations that are not actually dangerous.

While many will understand the concept of hypervigilance very well from personal experience, here's a very simple example.

A person who has experienced a car accident that left a traumatic impact on their subconscious may become easily triggered by the sound of car horns. Thus, a relatively mundane occurrence becomes something that activates a stress response. We are 'vigilant' when it's not really necessary in a practical sense.

This constant stress response is simply something an average person cannot (or should not) be wired to deal with on a day-to-day basis. In turn, this pressure necessitates a release, and escape.

This is how substances can enter the picture.

## Managing Our Emotions In the Face of Trauma

Emotional dysregulation refers to difficulties in managing and regulating emotions, leading to intense, overwhelming, and sometimes unpredictable emotional reactions. As mentioned above, this intensity can simply be unsustainable for most. The relief or distraction one can feel from their constant processing of trauma can become an extremely strong draw for continued use of a substance.

For people with PTSD and trauma, emotional dysregulation is a very common symptom, as they work daily to cope with difficult and distressing memories and feelings. Coping strategies, or the ways in which individuals manage and respond to stress, can be helpful or harmful, depending on the coping mechanism used.

Some examples of coping strategies that can be harmful and contribute to the development of bad habits include:

Substance abuse: Using drugs or alcohol to numb emotional pain or escape from distressing memories.

Self-harm: Engaging in self-destructive behaviors such as cutting or burning oneself.

Avoidance: Avoiding people, places, or situations that trigger traumatic memories, which can lead to social isolation and further emotional challenges.

Aggression: Using anger and aggression to cope with intense emotions, which can damage relationships and lead to further emotional dysregulation.

# 4. WHAT ARE SOME OF THE ESTABLISHED WAYS TO TREAT TRAUMA?

In the journey towards healing from trauma, it is crucial to uncover and address the core issues that lie beneath the surface. A variety of methods have been developed and utilized by mental health professionals and alternative therapists to facilitate this process. So let's explore some of the most common and promising methods for identifying and working through the roots of trauma, along with examples to illustrate their effectiveness.

*Traditional Talk Therapy*

Talk therapy, also known as psychotherapy, has long been the cornerstone of mental health treatment. And it continues to be instrumental in helping people heal.

It involves working with a mental health professional to explore thoughts, feelings, and behaviors related to traumatic experiences. Through guided conversations, individuals gain insights into their thought patterns and emotional responses, which can help them process and integrate traumatic memories. For example, a person who experienced childhood abuse may find it helpful to discuss their feelings of shame and guilt with a therapist, allowing them to reframe their perspective and move towards healing.

*Cognitive Behavioral Therapy (CBT)*

CBT is a popular form of talk therapy that focuses on identifying and changing negative thought patterns and behaviors related to trauma. By learning to recognize and challenge these patterns, individuals can develop healthier coping mechanisms and reduce the impact of trauma on their daily lives. In one example, a person with PTSD from a car accident might work with a therapist to identify the thoughts that trigger their anxiety, such as "I'm not safe," and replace them with more balanced thoughts like "Accidents are rare, and I can take precautions to stay safe."

*Eye Movement Desensitization and Reprocessing (EMDR)*

EMDR is a specialized form of therapy designed specifically to treat trauma. It involves the use of bilateral stimulation, such as eye movements, to help individuals process and reframe traumatic memories. EMDR has been shown to be particularly effective in treating PTSD and other trauma-related disorders.

For instance, a veteran suffering from combat-related PTSD might find relief through EMDR sessions, as the bilateral stimulation can help their brain reprocess the traumatic memories and reduce the intensity of their emotional reactions.

*Hypnotherapy*

Perhaps the most successful of the 'talk' therapies, hypnotherapy involves guiding individuals into a deeply relaxed state, allowing them to access their subconscious mind. In this state, they can explore and process traumatic memories that may be hidden or repressed. Hypnotherapy can be an effective way to uncover the roots of trauma and facilitate healing on a deep level. For example, a person struggling with unexplained panic attacks might discover, through hypnosis, that they had a near-drowning experience as a child, and by processing this memory, their panic attacks could subside.

## Somatic Therapies

Somatic therapies focus on the connection between the mind and body in the healing process.

Techniques such as Somatic Experiencing and Sensorimotor Psychotherapy involve working with physical sensations and movements to release the stored energy of traumatic experiences and promote integration and healing. A person who experienced physical assault might benefit from somatic therapy by learning to recognize and release the tension held in their body as a result of the trauma, ultimately finding relief from chronic pain and anxiety.

## Art and Expressive Therapies

Art, music, dance, and other forms of expressive therapies offer a creative and non-verbal way to explore and process traumatic experiences. These approaches can be particularly beneficial for those who have difficulty verbalizing their emotions or accessing memories through traditional talk therapy. A survivor of sexual abuse, for example, might find solace in painting or drawing images that represent their feelings, allowing them to process the trauma in a way that feels safe and therapeutic.

*Mindfulness and Meditation*

Mindfulness and meditation practices can help individuals develop a greater awareness of their thoughts, feelings, and bodily sensations. This increased self-awareness can provide valuable insights into the underlying issues related to trauma and create a space for healing and personal growth. By practicing mindfulness and meditation, individuals can learn to observe their thoughts and emotions without judgment, allowing them to gain a deeper understanding of their trauma and its impact on their lives. For instance, someone dealing with the emotional aftermath of a natural disaster might use mindfulness techniques to observe and accept their feelings of fear and loss, ultimately finding a sense of peace and resilience.

Group Therapy

Group therapy offers a supportive environment for individuals to share their experiences and work through their trauma with others who have faced similar challenges. The sense of community and understanding that emerges in group therapy can be incredibly validating and empowering. A person who lost a loved one to a terminal illness might find comfort in a grief support group, where they can share their feelings, learn from others' experiences, and develop coping strategies for navigating their loss.

## Psychodrama

Psychodrama is an experiential therapy that encourages individuals to reenact and explore traumatic experiences in a safe and controlled environment. By physically and emotionally engaging with their memories, individuals can gain new perspectives on their experiences and release pent-up emotions. For example, a person who grew up in an abusive household might participate in a psychodrama session to confront and express their anger towards their abusive parent, allowing them to process and move beyond their past.

## Plant Medicines and Psychedelic-Assisted Therapy

The use of plant substances such as Ibogaine, or psychedelics like MDMA and psilocybin, has gained increasing attention in recent years for their potential to help individuals access and process deep-rooted trauma. Under the guidance of trained professionals, these substances can induce profound emotional and spiritual experiences that facilitate healing and personal growth.

For instance, a person struggling with unresolved trauma from a violent assault might find that an Ibogaine-assisted therapy session allows them to confront and process the event in a way that traditional therapy could not.

Each of these methods offers a unique approach to uncovering and addressing the core issues of trauma. While some individuals might find success with one particular method, others may benefit from a combination of approaches. The key is to remain open to exploring different options and working with mental health professionals to find the most effective path towards healing and personal growth.

In the case of our facility, we have had the honor of being able to successfully treat over 350 of the most severe cases of trauma we had ever seen, and it is this, that now brings us to our description of our healing methods.

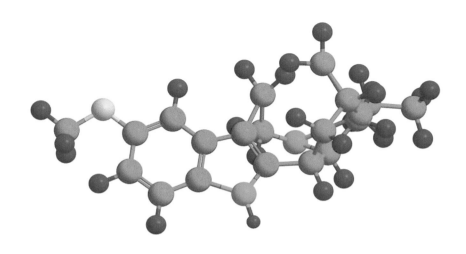

# 5. THE GIFT OF IBOGAINE

For many, the old ways of trying to help people with trauma were like using a band-aid for a broken arm – they just weren't enough.

Talking about problems helped a little, but it didn't always reach the deep-down fears and hurts. And medicine and therapies could make people feel less sad or worried, but it didn't fix the root of the problem. It was like turning down the volume of a noisy room instead of finding out why it's noisy in the first place.

Here's an example of how trauma affects someone in a practical sense: Let's talk about a person named Alex. Alex was in a car accident a few years ago. He seemed okay afterward, but he started having trouble sleeping and would get really jumpy at loud noises. He didn't understand why because he didn't remember being scared during the accident. That's because the trauma of the accident snuck into his subconscious. It was like a ghost in his house that he couldn't see but could feel.

So let's make simply the only true way to allow an individual to move forward from trauma, in a way that they can actually feel better permanently. We must stimulate the subconscious, which goes beyond the physical brain, revisit the traumatic event or events, bring all elements of the repressed trauma into the view of the conscious mind, to allow the individual's entire essence to fully witness and understand that the event is in the past, is over, and is no longer a threat to them.

What's the relationship between with ibogaine and trauma?

Ibogaine, when administered by a skilled practitioner, is like a special key that can unlock the safe of our subconscious. When people use it the right way, with doctors and support staff monitoring carefully, it can help them face their trauma. It's not like a magic pill that makes everything perfect, but it's as close as we've gotten in this world, as it can give people the chance to understand their fears and start to heal in a way no other form of therapy can.

Let's take a step back and give an idea of the power of ibogaine.

Of all the outstanding achievements of science and medicine, as of yet, one remains elusive:

We cannot build a living cell from scratch.

Even though all the components might be present, the ability to construct a cell truly from just its separate elements continues to elude us.

Oh, to be sure, science has made amazing advances in this area, but always with a starting point of using another functioning cell first.

What can we take away from this?

Well, simply, we can appreciate the wonder and power of nature to still have the answers to mysteries that are beyond our medical and scientific reach.

What is that spark that gives life...life? What allows an otherwise simple mechanism like a cell to replicate, divide into 2, 4, 6, 8, 32.... ?

And what happens when that spark in every cell is working 724 trillion times within our body?

The power of the human body is dizzying.

We trust it to make sense of the world, keep us aware of our surroundings, feel and connect with everything that is important to us.

And we trust it to execute unimaginable amounts of physiological processes every second.

The immune system is a part of this vast tapestry, and when working at full capacity, it can identify intrusions, seek out harmful elements, and keep us functioning at peak performance.

Too much of modern western medicine is focused on introducing external factors into the body to 'treat' or 'manage' the symptoms of issues.

But as Western society gradually wakes up to ancient and forgotten remedies, we are seeing a renewed appreciation for the efficiency of our body's own processes.

We combine the best of contemporary science and modern research with a deep respect for the human body, taking, whenever possible, a 'light touch' approach, and never interfering when we feel one's own psyche can do a better job at helping individuals heal.

## *Our Process in Treatment*

As we've now seen thoroughly so far in the book, trauma has been shown to be an underlying cause of many of contemporary society's ailments, from anxiety to executive burnout, to substance abuse, and beyond. And it's all rooted in the relationship between our subconscious and conscious minds. So at last, how do we leverage this knowledge and experience to actually *treat* people, in a permanent way?

In the past 15 years, the team at our center has been studying the science of trauma, and have developed a clear methodology that treats the roots of trauma, and subsequently, many other pathologies and conditions.

Here at Ibogaine by David Dardashti, we promote holistic health, and have had the fortune of achieving remarkable results for executive burnout, anxiety, trauma, and more.

Today, our all-inclusive treatments are sought after by hundreds of clients per month, who visit our center in Playa del Carmen, Mexico, and emerge with a new lease on life, and a new understanding of their trauma, how to move forward, and the freedom from habits and behaviors that were hindering them.

After over 15 years of treating individuals on a range of symptoms, we are deeply moved by the results we are seeing with our in-house combination of therapy and natural treatments to reach the root of trauma.

We are continuing to show people considering the treatment, that what we do is not 'too good to be true', but far from it.

The philosophy of the center is based on a series of core tenets:

1. The body's immune system has amazing healing capabilities, the sophistication of which has yet to be replicated by science.

2. The subconscious holds a record of all our traumas, capabilities & memories.

3. There are many differences between the functions of the conscious and subconscious mind.

4. It is natural for individuals to repress and archive experiences over the course of one's life.

5. The body executes trillions of processes every second.

6. The conscious mind is only aware of a small fraction of the processes happening in your body and brain at any given moment.

Based on these facts, we and our team have developed a carefully-executed series of treatments, combining traditional therapy with tools such as ibogaine, both in microdose and full doses, to unlock the immune system's own healing processes.

In recent years, tools like this have gained fame for its effectiveness on treating substance abuse such as severe opiate addiction, our team have gone far beyond this application and have developed successful protocols for treating things such as executive burnout, anxiety, and of course, trauma.

Publicly-available research, and the our Center's long-standing history both affirm: Ibogaine Hydrochloride helps people gain an introspective experience on their past, and helps unlock the subconscious information, so that it can be properly processed. In doing so, people are able to understand how the events in their lives have contributed to their present situation.

From there, we and his team incorporate techniques such as sound healing, connection with nature, as well as traditional therapy, to help guests emerge from treatment rejuvenated. The [testimonials](#) are clear, and successfully-treated clients range from all walks of life.

"This clinic helped save my life," says Whitney, one of our thousands of clients. "I had no idea where my life was going until I received treatment. I would recommend this treatment to anyone struggling with addiction and trauma, and David's facility was better than I could have ever imagined."

Individuals who are considering treatment are encouraged to reach out by phone for a brief consultation that can determine whether the Impulse Center is right for their needs. This applies to anyone suffering from severe anxiety, executive burnout, PTSD, and substance abuse.

As we've seen at length, Trauma is the result of past experiences that leave a person struggling to access suppressed memories, like an incomplete picture. The mind tried and tried to complete it, but can't access all the information required.

The most effective means for a person to deal with trauma is to internalize and relive the events in the past. We employ a proprietary technique that activates and accesses the subconscious history of trauma, and allows people to see the full picture of their past suffering.

# 6. CASE STUDIES: UNRAVELING THE THREADS OF A HIDDEN PAST

Let's take a deeper dive into a personal story about how an individual may actually find their way into addressing their trauma, and how it can be expunged from their inner mind.

*Names and details have been changed to protect privacy.

Jessica was a vibrant, ambitious woman in her early thirties. Outwardly, she seemed to have it all - a successful career, a loving partner, and a close circle of friends. Yet, beneath the surface, she struggled with a constant undercurrent of anxiety, self-doubt, and a nagging sense of emptiness. Despite her achievements, she could never quite shake the feeling that something essential was missing from her life.

As a child, Jessica had been raised in a seemingly idyllic home. Her parents were loving and supportive, and she and her younger sister, Emily, were inseparable. However, there was a hazy, indistinct memory from her childhood that occasionally surfaced in her dreams - a memory that left her feeling uneasy and unsettled. Though she could never recall the details of this event, she knew it was somehow connected to the persistent emotional turmoil that had haunted her for as long as she could remember.

Over the years, Jessica had sought help from various therapists and counselors, hoping to find relief from her emotional pain. Although she had made progress in managing her anxiety and improving her self-esteem, the core issue - that enigmatic childhood memory - remained locked away, seemingly beyond her reach. No matter how many therapists she consulted or coping strategies she tried, the truth remained stubbornly hidden in the depths of her subconscious mind.

It was during a casual conversation with a friend that Jessica first learned about the potential of Ibogaine to help individuals access and heal from deeply repressed trauma. Intrigued by the idea and desperate for answers, she began researching the treatment and eventually decided to embark on an Ibogaine therapy journey.

The Ibogaine session was unlike anything Jessica had ever experienced. As the substance took effect, her mind was transported to a vivid, dream-like state where long-buried memories and emotions began to emerge. She found herself revisiting a childhood scene, playing in her family's backyard with Emily. As the memory unfolded, she saw her seven-year-old self being approached by a trusted neighbor - a man she had always considered a kind and friendly presence in her life.

As the scene continued to play out, Jessica watched in horror as the neighbor led her younger self into a secluded area of the garden, where he proceeded to sexually assault her. The shock of this revelation was overwhelming, and she felt a torrent of emotions - anger, sadness, and a deep sense of betrayal. The memory had been so effectively repressed that she had no conscious recollection of the event, even though it had profoundly impacted her emotional well-being throughout her life.

With the help of the Ibogaine therapy and the guidance of her skilled facilitators, Jessica was able to confront and process the emotions associated with this traumatic experience.

The emotional release that followed was intense, and she felt as though a heavy weight had been lifted from her shoulders. As the session came to an end, she realized that she had finally found the missing piece of the puzzle - the key to understanding and healing the emotional wounds that had held her captive for so many years.

In the weeks and months that followed her Ibogaine experience, Jessica worked diligently to integrate the insights she had gained into her daily life.

We've always continued to recommend that people continue their journey into self-exploration. She sought out trauma-informed therapy to help her navigate the challenges of recovery and attended support groups to connect with others who had faced similar experiences. Slowly but surely, she began to rebuild her life on a foundation of self-compassion, understanding, and emotional freedom.

Jessica's journey through the shadows of her past was not an easy one, but it ultimately led her to a place of profound healing and transformation. By facing these repressed moments head-on, the body was, as we've previously mentioned, able to complete the ever-important complete picture of one's self, and create a sensation of overall peace with the past.

*Christine's Transformation*

Nothing can be a clearer example about the subconscious's role in storing trauma than Christine's.

Perhaps so, because her story is accompanied by some beautiful visual representation of her experience.

Over the years in treating individuals, almost every story profoundly touches our hearts and minds. Christine's is one such story, and it tells us of a journey that not only speaks to her personal struggles but also sheds a crystal clear light on the healing potential of ibogaine.

Christine's battle began when she was just four years old. She faced the challenges of Obsessive-Compulsive Disorder (OCD) and deep-rooted trauma, a journey that many can relate to, yet each experience is unique.

What made Christine's story stand out was how she expressed her inner turmoil. She turned to painting, a way to show what words often couldn't. Her artwork was a window into her soul, each piece telling a story of pain, confusion, and a longing for understanding.

As we saw earlier in the book, trauma is like a series of incomplete pictures taken by the brain. These snapshots capture moments of intense emotion but often miss the full story. Over time, these fragments can become a confusing puzzle, a source of ongoing pain and misunderstanding.

"I started making art heavily about four years ago because I just didn't feel right. I knew something was wrong," she describes.

In Christine's paintings, we saw these fragments. One particularly striking piece seemed to show a split personality. But we understood it wasn't about having multiple personalities. It was her way of depicting the fragmentation of her own experiences, a visual metaphor for her inner conflict. "I was always so anxious and stressed out, and my brain would just never stop," she continues.

As she progressed in life, this outlet became her lifeline, and her connection to the inner worlds that, as we saw earlier, were just out of reach to her conscious mind.

Another painting brought us closer to her childhood experiences, particularly her relationship with her mother. The emotions in this painting were complex and deep, reflecting the impact of her mother's struggles on her young mind.

Our journey with Christine through ibogaine treatment was about piecing together these fragments. We aimed to help her access her subconscious, to bring those hidden memories to the surface, and to understand them in their entirety. This understanding is crucial for healing, for it allows the mind to recognize that the traumatic event is over.

Through ibogaine therapy, Christine embarked on a transformative journey. It was a path of deep introspection, of facing fears, and of finding peace. This treatment, which uses a powerful plant medicine, represents a significant shift from traditional approaches to mental health.

My art was like my subconscious trying to show me what was

wrong with me, what I was going through. All my art was showing me about my trauma that I went through, and it was like my subconscious self trying to tell me what was wrong with me, and I didn't even know that I was doing that. So yeah, now it all makes sense. Thank God; thank you."

In Jessica and Christine's cases, and with thousands more seen first-hand through this treatment, Ibogaine offers a powerful, transformative experience that can help individuals access and heal from deeply repressed trauma. Its ability to penetrate the unconscious mind, facilitate emotional release, and promote reintegration and healing has made it an invaluable tool for those seeking lasting recovery and personal growth.

Here's an analogy of how our methodology can access the trauma more effectively (or more quickly) than many other methods. The trauma, as we've seen, is tangled up in the very fabric of the brain and the subconscious. Imagine a ball of yarn the size of your brain made out of thousands of threads, each one, meters long.

A few of those threads are part of the unresolved trauma, but they're tangled across the entire expanse of your brain. Now choose one and pull.

Do you think you'd get it all? What about the rest? Even if you knew which threads they were, it would be impossible to manually complete the task of pulling them out.

We've seen how natural substances are considered a viable option to treat trauma; now we'll dive specifically into the actual science behind Ibogaine, demystifying its complex mechanisms of action and shedding light on how it impacts the brain and facilitates profound healing.

Get ready to unravel some more of the mysteries of this powerful, transformative substance.

## *So What is the Science of how Our Treatment Works?*

As we've seen throughout this book, for many individuals, unresolved trauma lies at the root of their struggles with addiction, mental health issues, or unfulfilling patterns in their lives.

These deeply repressed memories and emotions often remain buried, exerting a powerful influence on their thoughts, behaviors, and relationships, but the only true solution is to reach into the subconscious and wrench them out, to face the healing power of the sunlight, so the trauma can be transformed from that mile-long, deep, amorphous and scary presence, into one, small and minute, crystal clear piece of information, that the conscious mind can comprehend in only a few seconds, instead of hours or years. It's about seeing what happened in a simple way, and understanding that it's completely over.

By having this clarity, the individual now has the freedom, just like with any memory, to recall it in simply a few seconds, instead of the constant perception that there is an unending thread that needs to be unraveled. (Which often simply creates more trauma as they continue to seek and recall things which may not have even been true.) It's like playing a game of broken telephone with your own brain. Your brain tries to tell yourself the story, over and over, and each time, the story changes, shifts, adapts along with your anxiety about it.

This is why individuals can do years of therapy, work hard to make advancements, follow all the right steps, and still feel like they're not making progress.

Why? Because as the conscious attempts to talk through it over and over, more current anxieties mix in with original trauma, and even small things that happen in the day-to-day, creating a snowball effect where the original trauma appears to be larger and more and more insurmountable than it ever was.

So ibogaine, this wonderful natural substance derived from the Tabernanthe iboga plant, holds the potential to unearth these hidden traumas, shrinking the 'extra long thread' so to speak so it's short and manageable.

Just like a great hypnotist can help a person access the truth about what's hidden in their subconscious, pure ibogaine, administered by a seasoned expert, can be the tool that can, in only a few seconds, vs years of discussing the problem, can make the trauma visible, understood, and clear.

Now, many people ask us, 'how long is an ibogaine treatment'? If it only takes a few seconds to initially witness and understand and wipe out the mystery of trauma, what other elements are part of the process?

What actually happens in the brain? Let's explore the extraordinary science of how Ibogaine can be that tool that allows us to access these specific moments of trauma so perfectly.

### *Phase 1: Accessing the Unconscious Mind:*

We penetrate the depths of the unconscious mind, accessing memories and emotions that have been long buried or forgotten. During a session, individuals often experience vivid visions, dream-like states, or intense emotions that can reveal hidden aspects of their psyche. This deep exploration of the subconscious mind allows them to confront and process repressed traumas, which is an essential step in the healing process.

### *Phase 2: Emotional Release and Catharsis:*

As repressed memories and emotions come to the surface during a session, individuals have the opportunity to confront them and release the emotional pain that has been locked away for years, even decades. This emotional release can be an intensely cathartic experience, allowing users to let go of the burdens they have been carrying and make space for healing, growth, and self-acceptance. By shedding the weight of past traumas, individuals can begin to rebuild their lives on a foundation of emotional freedom and inner peace, all happening within a very short time.

## *Phase 3: Reintegration and Healing:*

Following the emotional release and catharsis that occurs during a session, individuals must reintegrate the insights they have gained into their daily lives. This process involves reexamining their beliefs, values, and behaviors, as well as making necessary changes to support their ongoing healing and personal growth.

Reintegration may include seeking therapy or counseling, engaging in mindfulness practices, or developing new, healthier coping strategies. By incorporating the lessons learned during their experience, individuals can move forward with a renewed sense of purpose, resilience, and self-awareness.

## *The Importance of Support and Aftercare:*

It is crucial to acknowledge that this therapy is not a panacea for all emotional wounds. While many have experienced a successful treatment as a one-time solution to deeply rooted trauma, we always know there is more to be done.

The process of healing from repressed trauma is often complex and multifaceted, requiring ongoing support and care.

Following a session, a person may feel as though they've been given a new lease on life, and the power to act freely with confidence. Put another way, a treatment, administered correctly, puts an individual at 'the top of the hill' looking at their new potential for life, rather than being part of them struggling to climb up it.

However, it is vital for individuals to engage in a comprehensive aftercare program that may include therapy, support groups, or other resources to help them navigate the challenges of recovery and maintain the progress they have made.

No matter how amazing a neuro-stimulus treatment is, it is crucial that people remember the amount of change they have been through, and to honor and be gracious about the fact their brain has essentially been rewired in a better way.

*What can the treatment really do for a person?*

First, a bit about its overall capabilities. From reducing drug cravings to improving mental clarity and emotional stability, our treatment has the potential to be a powerful tool in the fight against addiction. This is perhaps the most publicized aspect of its usefulness.

But it goes far beyond this. Particularly, we've focused and harnessed on ibogaine's powerful ability to reach deep into the psyche and address further root causes for unwanted behaviors.

The reason Ibogaine is so effective in treating trauma lies in its unique impact on the brain. It acts as a powerful psychoactive substance that enables users to access repressed memories and emotions, facilitating a deep self-exploration that can lead to profound healing. Let's discuss ibogaine's unique mechanism of action and how it relates to the brain, and allows us to delve into the subconscious.

*Neurotransmitter Modulation:*

At the core of the therapy's effectiveness lies its ability to modulate various neurotransmitters in the brain, such as dopamine, serotonin, and glutamate.

By regulating these key chemicals, the treatment helps to restore balance in the brain's reward system, which is often disrupted in individuals suffering from addiction or mental health issues. This action not only aids in alleviating withdrawal symptoms but also reduces cravings and negative thought patterns, paving the way for a healthier, more balanced state of mind.

Another critical aspect of the treatment's healing power is its capacity to stimulate neuroplasticity, the brain's ability to create new connections and pathways. This process allows for the reorganization of thought patterns and behaviors, enabling individuals to gain new perspectives on past experiences and make lasting changes in their lives. By promoting cognitive flexibility, we empower people to break free from destructive habits and embrace healthier ways of coping with stress and emotional pain.

*Spiritual Connection and Growth:*

Many who undergo the therapy report a heightened sense of spiritual connection, both to themselves and the world around them.

This deepened sense of spirituality often helps individuals find meaning and purpose in their lives, making it easier to let go of past traumas and embrace a more hopeful, fulfilling future.

We understand that for those embarking on a journey towards healing and self-discovery, it can be both challenging and intimidating. But by understanding the science behind this remarkable process, we hope to provide you with the knowledge and reassurance you need to make informed decisions about your healing journey.

*Cognitive Reorganization:*

Ibogaine stimulates the brain's neuroplasticity, promoting new connections and pathways. This process helps individuals reframe their perspective on past traumatic experiences, enabling them to integrate the lessons and move forward with a renewed sense of self.

One of the most remarkable aspects of Ibogaine therapy is its ability to promote cognitive reorganization, a process that allows individuals to restructure their thought patterns and behaviors in a meaningful and lasting way. This transformative effect is particularly significant for those struggling with addiction, mental health issues, or unresolved trauma. Let's explore how Ibogaine facilitates cognitive reorganization and the lasting impact it can have on personal growth and healing.

*Rewiring the Brain:*

Ibogaine stimulates the brain's neuroplasticity, which refers to the brain's ability to adapt and reorganize itself by forming new neural connections and pathways. This adaptability is crucial for learning, memory, and recovering from brain injuries or damage. When individuals undergo Ibogaine therapy, the enhanced neuroplasticity allows them to rewire their brain, essentially "rewriting" old, unhelpful thought patterns and replacing them with healthier, more constructive ones.

*Breaking Free from Unhealthy Thought Patterns:*

Many individuals struggling with addiction or trauma develop cognitive distortions or unhealthy thought patterns that contribute to their suffering. These distortions can include negative self-talk, catastrophizing, or black-and-white thinking. By promoting cognitive reorganization, Ibogaine helps break the cycle of these harmful thoughts, allowing users to develop a more balanced, rational, and positive outlook on their lives.

*Enhancing Self-Awareness and Emotional Intelligence:*

Cognitive reorganization also fosters a greater sense of self-awareness and emotional intelligence. Through the Ibogaine experience, individuals gain insight into their thoughts, emotions, and behaviors, enabling them to identify and modify any maladaptive patterns. This heightened self-awareness empowers them to better understand their triggers, manage their emotions, and respond more effectively to challenging situations.

*Facilitating Lasting Behavioral Change:*

The cognitive reorganization induced by Ibogaine therapy paves the way for lasting behavioral change. By reshaping thought patterns and enhancing self-awareness, individuals can develop healthier coping strategies, break free from the grip of addiction, and maintain long-term recovery. This lasting transformation is particularly significant, as it equips individuals with the tools and resilience needed to face future challenges without resorting to self-destructive habits.

In conclusion, the cognitive reorganization facilitated by Ibogaine therapy is a critical aspect of its healing potential. By rewiring the brain, breaking free from unhealthy thought patterns, enhancing self-awareness, and fostering lasting behavioral change, Ibogaine empowers individuals to overcome addiction, heal from trauma, and embark on a path of personal growth and lasting recovery.

*Accessing Repressed Memories and Emotional Release:*

Because of all of the above, during an Ibogaine session, individuals often experience vivid visions and dream-like states that can bring repressed memories to the surface. By accessing these long-forgotten memories, they can confront and process the emotions associated with them, leading to a newfound understanding of their past and present selves.

Ibogaine has the power to unlock emotions that have been buried for years, even decades. It allows users to confront these feelings head-on and release them, resulting in a significant reduction in anxiety, depression, and other symptoms related to unresolved trauma.

*Safety and Precautions:*

Although our process has shown tremendous potential for healing trauma, it is essential to approach it with caution. This powerful substance, while suitable for almost all people, should only be administered by experienced professionals with both a deep understanding of its physiological effects, and an impeccable track-record of using it to help individuals heal, and most importantly, remain successfully improved 90 - 95% from past issues.

Addiction is a complex and multifaceted issue that affects individuals from all walks of life.

People often tell us that they feel more intelligent, they can think better, they can remember the past more completely, and many of them call up parents and family members they haven't spoken to for years, and ask for forgiveness with an open spirit and willingness to reconnect. It's as if the decades of pride, resentment, and anger have melted away.

*But Can Our Treatment Really
Help Almost Anyone?*

Over the past year, we've had the pleasure of participating in several psychedelic research events, including the Psychedelic Science conference in Denver Colorado, and having meaningful conversations with an overwhelming amount of people, both in the medical/therapeutic fields, doctors specialized in different disciplines, and individuals themselves seeking healing through natural substances.

Among the many questions people had about ibogaine was "Can the treatment really cure addiction to [insert substance here]? Can it cure addiction to [insert other substance here]?"

These questions reflect a common curiosity about the true effectiveness of ibogaine therapy in treating different types of addiction, often focusing on the specific prescription or illicit drug in question.

The answer, well, is yes.

But it's not so much about the substance the individual is addicted to; it's about the internal mechanisms that are causing the repetitive and unwanted behavior.

YES, ibogaine, in and of itself, boasts wonderful capabilities to completely cut withdrawals, boost neuroplasticity and help reset the nervous system. In this regard, there is very little else on the planet that is showing such effectiveness in being able to repair neurons, reconnect the synapses, and affect permanent positive change in the brain.

And that's what makes people feel that they've been given some miraculous solution to their problems.

But the art and experience involved with how we administer ibogaine, the 99.9% purity we use, and the way we combine it with other treatments to treat trauma is where the ability to *keep* people off their substances is truly achieved. After over 3,000 successfully treated ibogaine patients, this is what we definitively know.

*Finding the Root Cause*

Regardless of the substance, the key to successful addiction treatment lies in addressing the root trauma that fuels addictive behaviors. While it is true that different substances require tailored protocols and individualized treatment to account for the physiological particularities of each drug, there is a common thread that runs through successful addiction treatment: addressing the root trauma.

Through the profound healing and transformative power of ibogaine therapy, individuals can access their subconscious, confront repressed memories, and experience a spiritual moment of awareness that paves the way for true healing and recovery.

At the core of addiction lies unresolved trauma. Traumatic experiences can have a profound impact on an individual's mental, emotional, and physical well-being, often leading to a range of issues including addiction. Trauma can take many forms, from childhood abuse and neglect to the aftermath of a traumatic event. These experiences create deep-seated wounds that drive individuals to seek solace in substances as a coping mechanism. In a worst case, it can lead individuals to deep depression, all the way to suicide.

Unresolved trauma can manifest in various ways, such as feelings of shame, guilt, or low self-worth. It can also result in emotional and psychological imbalances, including anxiety, depression, and post-traumatic stress disorder (PTSD). Additionally, trauma can disrupt the healthy development of coping mechanisms, interpersonal skills, and emotional regulation, making individuals more susceptible to addictive behaviors.

The connection between trauma and addiction is often overlooked, and is one of the reasons that those seeking to use ibogaine as a 'blunt instrument' to cut addiction, often find themselves coming up short in the long run, leaving patients part of the way toward healing, but unfortunately liable to backslide.

It is absolutely vital to recognize that addiction is not solely a matter of willpower or moral failing. It is a complex interplay of biological, psychological, and social factors, with trauma acting as a significant catalyst.

After speaking with thousands of people that we've had the honor of treating, I personally interview them to determine whether there is a repressed trauma, (and as we've seen earlier, in many caes they are completely unaware of) and if so, how severe it is.

By addressing the underlying trauma, we can unravel the intricate web of addiction and pave the way for lasting recovery.

*The Expanded Power of the Healing Potential*

While the substance is often associated with treating specific substances, such as opioids or stimulants, the truth is that it can effectively address addiction to any substance. This is because the key lies not in the substance itself, but in treating the root trauma that drives addictive behaviors, such as gambling and sex addiction.

By accessing the subconscious mind, it unlocks repressed memories and emotions, allowing individuals to confront and process the traumatic events that have shaped their addiction. This powerful tool provides a unique opportunity for individuals to gain deep insights, experience profound catharsis, and release the emotional burdens that have kept them trapped in addictive patterns.

## Personalized Treatment for Lasting Results

While this therapy forms the core of our treatment approach, it is not a one-size-fits-all solution. Each individual's journey is unique, and we understand the importance of tailoring treatment to meet their specific needs. Through years of extensive research and expertise, I and my medical team have developed over 350 protocols that consider a multitude of factors to achieve consistently excellent results.

Our approach involves combining our treatment with a comprehensive range of therapies and modalities that support the healing process. This holistic approach takes into account the individual's physical, emotional, and spiritual well-being, ensuring a comprehensive and personalized treatment plan. By addressing the root trauma and providing the necessary support, we empower individuals to break free from the grip of addiction and embark on a journey of lasting recovery.

Regardless of the substance, the answer to whether we can treat addiction is resoundingly 'yes.' By combining personalized protocols, a supportive environment, and a holistic approach, we empower individuals to overcome their addiction and reclaim their lives.

## *Anyone can be affected by trauma*

Trauma is a common occurrence in our modern world, affecting millions of people across the globe. If you're reading this, you may be one of them. If so, perhaps you're actively hiding it - but you are not alone, and as we've shown in this book, respressing and running from it simply does not work.

In our roster of past clients, we have dealt with people from all walks of life, and among them, have been many high-level and powerful executives and businesspeople. Over the years, we have maintained strict confidentiality of their identities, and through our process of healing, have been able to pull them away from extreme anxiety, stress depression and suffering due to their own traumas.

Trauma knows no race, class, color, or social status, and can, and does, indeed affect anyone.

Traumatic experiences can be caused by a wide range of events, such as natural disasters, accidents, violence, abuse, and as we've seen earlier, bullying, but no matter the cause, they can all have long-lasting effects on mental and physical health.

While some individuals are able to recover from trauma with the support of family, friends, and mental health professionals, for far too many, others may struggle with more negative effects, such as post-traumatic stress disorder and a host of other additional challenges.

Among these, one of the most prevailing is substance abuse or addiction. Research has shown that individuals with PTSD or trauma are more likely to develop substance use disorders than those without, and the co-occurrence of these conditions can make treatment more complex.

But why? What is it about the relationship between addiction and trauma makes them so intertwined?

By developing healthy coping strategies and seeking support, individuals can better manage their emotions and avoid the harmful impact of bad habits.

**Support systems to cope with trauma and addiction**

Beyond our own treatment, which we've shown to have an exteremly high success rate, developing a strong support system can provide individuals with the resources and encouragement they need to manage their symptoms and avoid relapse. Here are some examples of support systems and relapse prevention strategies:

*Therapy and Counseling*: Therapy and counseling can help individuals with PTSD and addiction to understand the root causes of their symptoms and develop coping strategies to manage their emotions and behaviors. Various types of therapy, such as cognitive-behavioral therapy, trauma-focused therapy, and group therapy, can be helpful.

*Peer Support Groups:* Peer support groups can provide a sense of community and understanding for individuals with PTSD and addiction. Groups like Alcoholics Anonymous (AA) and Narcotics Anonymous (NA) provide a space for individuals to connect with others who have experienced similar challenges.

*Lifestyle Changes*: Developing healthy habits such as regular exercise, healthy eating, and getting enough sleep can help reduce symptoms of PTSD and addiction. These lifestyle changes can improve physical and mental health and reduce the risk of relapse.

*Self-Care*: Engaging in self-care activities such as meditation, mindfulness, or creative activities can provide a sense of relaxation and help reduce stress and anxiety.

*Relapse Prevention Planning*: Developing a relapse prevention plan can help individuals identify triggers and warning signs for relapse and develop strategies to avoid relapse. A relapse prevention plan can include strategies for managing triggers, engaging in healthy activities, and reaching out for support.

*Neuro-stimulus treatment*: Naturally, if a treatment can get right to the root of the trauma, and make it visible and manageable by the individual, this is absolutely ideal, and can help heal what might take years, in simply weeks or months.

Overall, building a strong support system and developing relapse prevention strategies can be instrumental in addressing the link between trauma, PTSD, and bad habits. By taking a proactive approach to managing symptoms and seeking support, individuals can work towards recovery and healing.

*Forgiveness and Trauma*

No matter what the treatment, or the regular steps one takes to move forward, there is one ultimate step that cannot be overlooked: forgiveness.

Forgiveness is a crucial piece of the puzzle towards healing and recovery for individuals who have experienced trauma.

More specifically, this involves forgiving oneself and others who may have caused the traumatic experience. But why? Well, put simply, forgiving oneself means acknowledging that the trauma is not their fault and releasing self-blame and self-punishment.

One important note: we have to recognize that forgiveness is not condoning or excusing the behavior of those who caused the trauma but rather a way of releasing the emotional burden of anger and resentment, allowing for emotional closure. Once complete, individuals can experience a sense of peace and freedom, and move beyond the trauma.

Forgiveness can bring many benefits to mental and emotional well-being, improving relationships and quality of life. Through therapy, self-reflection, and self-care, individuals can learn to forgive themselves and others and move towards a more hopeful and fulfilling future.

It's not easy, but it is an essential part of the healing journey and can help individuals reclaim their lives and move beyond the trauma.

## Unlocking the Potential of the Subconscious: A Summary of its Profound Power

The human mind is an incredible powerhouse, with the subconscious playing a crucial role in shaping our thoughts, emotions, and behaviors. While we often focus on the conscious mind, the vast and mysterious world of the subconscious holds the key to unlocking our true potential, impacting not only our physical well-being but also the depths of our soul.

### Diving into the Depths of the Subconscious

Our subconscious mind operates silently in the background, influencing our daily lives in ways we might not even realize. It is a storehouse of memories, emotions, and beliefs that have been accumulated throughout our lives. By tapping into the subconscious, we can uncover the hidden driving forces behind our actions, empowering us to break free from self-limiting beliefs and negative patterns.

*The Healing Power of the Subconscious Mind*

The subconscious mind has an incredible capacity to facilitate healing and personal growth. When we access and engage this powerful resource, we can accelerate the healing process by tapping into our body's natural ability to regenerate and repair itself. The subconscious mind can help us identify and release emotional blockages, allowing us to move past traumas and rediscover inner peace.

*The Connection Between Subconscious and Soul*

Our subconscious mind is not just a powerful tool for physical healing; it also holds the key to our spiritual well-being. By delving into the depths of our subconscious, we can uncover our soul's true purpose and gain a deeper understanding of ourselves and our place in the world. This spiritual connection can guide us towards a more fulfilling and meaningful life, filled with personal growth, self-discovery, and a profound sense of inner harmony.

*Unlocking Your Full Potential*

By understanding and embracing the power of the subconscious, we can unlock our full potential as human beings, both physically and spiritually. This journey into the depths of our minds can lead to profound insights and lasting transformation, enabling us to live our lives with greater clarity, purpose, and inner peace. So, take the first step towards unlocking the hidden power of your subconscious mind, and embark on a journey of self-discovery that can change the course of your life.

# 7. THE WIDESPREAD EFFECTS OF TRAUMA ON SOCIETY AS A WHOLE.

Trauma is like a shadow that follows us around. It's not just something one person feels; it's like a cold wind that can chill a whole town. In this chapter, we're going to talk about what happens when we don't look at this shadow, when we all pretend it's not there. It's like when everyone in a room hears a loud noise but no one talks about it. That's what we do with trauma in our world.

We've learned that there are ways to help people with trauma, ways that can work fast, like our neuro-stimulus treatment. It's like having a fast-acting medicine when you're sick. But what if we don't use that medicine? What if we keep going on, feeling bad, and never getting better?

When we keep doing the same thing over and over, it's like walking the same path until it's a deep groove in the ground. We've been walking around trauma, stepping over it, and now it's like a groove we can't get out of. But what does that do to us, to our friends, our families, and the places we live?

This chapter is like a list of what happens when that groove gets too deep. It's like when you ignore a small leak in a pipe. At first, it's just a drip, but then it can turn into a flood. We'll see how not talking about trauma can make people angry, confused, and sad. It's like if everyone in a town was carrying a heavy bag but no one put them down.

We'll look at real things that happen. Like how a whole neighborhood can feel scared if there's a lot of crime, or how people can get mad at each other when they don't understand what's going on. It's like when everyone's hungry and there's only a little food; people start to fight instead of helping each other.

But we won't just talk about the bad stuff. We'll also ask, "What if?" What if we started to actually understand and use the fast-acting natural treatments for our trauma? What if we stopped walking around the problem and faced it? It's like turning on a light in a dark room. Everything looks different when you can see.

Trauma is a big and heavy word, but it's really just about needing help to connect the dots. And helping can start with just seeing and saying, "Yes, this is real."

We're going to look at how trauma touches all of us, like a cold wind that gets into every house. And we'll see how we can warm things up, not just for one person, but for everyone. It's like sharing a fire on a cold day. It's better when we're all together.


## Inability to Face the Truth

In every corner of our lives, from the quiet of our homes to the buzz of our streets, trauma hides in plain sight. It's like a shadow that follows us, unseen but always there. What happens when this isn't just something we face alone, but something we all ignore together?

Think about the times we go online. The internet is full of information, but also full of lies. Why do we argue about things that aren't true? Why do we believe stories that make no sense? It's not just about being wrong; it's about not wanting to see the real problems we face. The internet can be a mirror, showing us not just what we think, but how we feel.

Why do we hold on to lies? Maybe the truth hurts too much. Maybe we've all been hurt in ways we don't want to admit. Online, we find places that tell us what we want to hear, not what we need to hear. It's easier that way, but it doesn't help us fix what's really wrong.

It's not just on the internet, either. Look at our leaders and the laws they make. Sometimes, they treat the symptoms of our problems, not the cause. They put a bandage on a wound that needs more care. What are we afraid to face? What hurts are we ignoring?

And what about the movies we watch, the games we play, the stories we tell? There's so much violence and pain. Is this because we're used to hurt? Or are we trying to forget our own pain by watching someone else's?

Ignoring the truth is like building a wall to keep out the bad stuff.

But when we do that, we also keep out the good. We can't grow or get better if we don't face what's wrong. We just keep making the same mistakes, feeling the same hurts.

So, how do we stop going in circles? First, we have to admit there's a problem. We have to be brave and look at the hard things. We have to see the hurt in our past and in each other's eyes. The first step to getting better is seeing what's wrong.

But seeing isn't enough. We have to do something about it. We need to talk to each other, learn about what hurts us, and find ways to make it better. We need to support laws that get to the heart of our problems, like making sure everyone can get help when they're feeling bad inside.

Not facing the truth is a sign that we're all hurt in some way. It shows we have work to do, not just alone, but all of us together.

Are we ready to do that work? Are we ready to stop ignoring the hurt and start fixing it?

In a world where it's hard to tell what's real, we all have to try harder to find the truth. It's not easy. It means facing things we'd rather not. But if we can do that, we can change things. We can heal not just ourselves, but our families and the whole world.

**Guilt about failing to act:**

Certainly, let's explore the theme of societal guilt and its impact on collective action:

Guilt. It has driven people to do great things, and driven people to near paralysis. But when we're talking about society as a whole, guilt is unfortunately an all-too-real result of unaddressed trauma.

And when this guilt is not merely personal but collective, it can suffocate a society's ability to act decisively, leading to a paralysis that hinders progress and exacerbates the very issues we feel guilty about.

Take, for instance, the environmental crisis. As a society, we are inundated with evidence of our role in climate change—melting ice caps, devastating wildfires, and extreme weather events. Yet, there's a pervasive sense of guilt about our individual and collective failure to act. How often do we hear of someone lamenting their carbon footprint, yet feeling powerless to make a difference? This guilt, while valid, can lead to inaction, as the magnitude of the problem seems to dwarf individual efforts.

Consider the social and political issues that ignite public debate. Issues like racial inequality, poverty, and healthcare disparities are often met with widespread acknowledgment of their urgency, yet action is slow. Society, it seems, is trapped in a cycle of guilt over past injustices and present failures, which ironically, hampers the very actions needed to fix these issues.

In many ways, we can get addicted to guilt. We often prefer identifying, distributing and absorbing guilt rather than solving the problems we're guilty about.

Why do we, as a society, feel guilty yet fail to act? Is it because the problems seem too big, too entrenched? Or is it because admitting guilt requires us to take responsibility, to step out of our comfort zones and make tangible changes?

The phenomenon of 'bystander apathy' is a stark example of this paralysis. When faced with an emergency, individuals often expect others to step in. This diffusion of responsibility can lead to tragic outcomes, as everyone waits for someone else to act. On a societal level, this translates to a collective shrug—acknowledging the problem but assuming it's someone else's to solve.

And what about the guilt that comes from privilege? The uncomfortable truth that some of us benefit from systems that oppress others? This guilt can be immobilizing, leading to performative acts of solidarity rather than meaningful change. It's easier to wear a pin, post a hashtag, or attend a rally than to engage in the sustained effort required to dismantle oppressive systems.

But guilt can also be transformative. It can push us to educate ourselves, to listen to those affected by the issues, and to take action in our communities. It can inspire us to vote, to volunteer, to advocate, and to change our habits. The key is to move beyond guilt as an endpoint and see it as a beginning—a call to action.

## Anger and Irritability

In a world where tempers seem to flare at the slightest provocation, we find ourselves in a society simmering with anger and irritability. It's like a spark that can easily ignite, spreading through communities and conversations, leaving a trail of discord and tension.

Why are we so angry? Is it because life has become more stressful, or have we just become less tolerant? The truth is, our anger often comes from a place of hurt, of unresolved issues that we carry with us. When one person snaps, it can set off a chain reaction. Have you noticed how one angry comment online can lead to a flood of heated replies?

Think about driving on a busy road. One person honks, and suddenly it's a chorus of frustration. But what are we achieving with this? Does it get us to our destination any faster, or does it just raise our blood pressure?

And it's not just on the roads or online. It's in our homes, our workplaces, our schools, and especially on the news. Why has the news become so negative? It's because that's what sells, that's the reaction that generates the most interaction. And it's not just you - this phenomenon affects us all.

We're quick to anger, quick to judge, and slow to understand. But what if we stopped for a moment? What if we asked ourselves why the other person might be upset? Could we turn our anger into something more productive?

Anger makes it hard to work together. It's tough to solve problems when everyone is shouting. Have you tried to have a conversation with someone who's angry? It's like talking to a brick wall.

According to Kabbalah, anger is one of the factors that moves us farther from our loved ones, farther from spirituality, and farther from the creator. It takes our natural mental understanding, and switches it off.

Anger literally reduces our intelligence. In short, anger makes us dumber.

In a community, when anger takes over, it's like a storm that never ends. It can ruin friendships, break down teamwork, and make neighbors turn against each other. But communities need to work like a team. What happens to a sports team when the players are fighting? They lose, right?

So, what can we do about all this anger? It starts with each of us. Can we take a deep breath before we respond? Can we think twice before we post that angry comment online? It's not easy, but it's important.

It can take years of practice, but we must each find a way to reduce our anger little by little every day. If that means simply taking a breath or going for a walk before confronting someone we're angry with, practicing self-control is crucial.

Because holding onto anger is like holding onto a hot coal. The only person who gets burned is you.

Anger and irritability can spread through a society, but so can kindness and understanding. It's up to us to decide which one we want to pass on. Do we want to live in a world where everyone is mad all the time, or do we want to try to make things better?

A society filled with anger is a society that's stuck. It's like a car with a flat tire; it can't go anywhere. But if we can fix that tire, if we can turn our anger into something good, then we can all move forward together.

Kabbalah describes anger as akin to idol worshiping. One's spiritual values can easily leave a person and he makes a decision in a way that's closer to a wild animal than an intelligent human.

The good news is that by simply practicing even a few seconds of self control, one can effectively raise their emotional IQ by fifty points.

It's like choosing to walk away from a fight. You're not giving up; you're choosing to win in a different way, and no one has to get hurt.

So, what can we do right now to pull out the weeds of anger in our society? We can start small. We can listen more and shout less. We can think about how our words affect others. We can be the calm voice in a room full of noise.

Stop honking, accept the traffic. Stop posting negative comments on social media. Stop criticizing the same things in a loved one over and over and try a different approach.

And when we ourselves mess up, because we all do, can we say sorry? Can we admit we were wrong? That's one of the hardest things to do, but it's also one of the most important. And apology doesn't make one weak, it makes you strong and honorable.

In the end, a society without anger isn't just a dream. It's something we can build, together. It starts with each of us, every day, in the small choices we make. We can choose to be kind, to be patient, to be the person who makes a difference.

Because when we look back, what do we want to see? A garden full of weeds or one full of flowers? The choice is ours, and it's a choice we make every day.

## Mental Confusion

In a world that's moving faster than ever, it's easy to feel lost in the whirlwind of information, opinions, and expectations. This feeling of being lost can create a fog in our minds, a kind of mental confusion that makes it hard to see where we're going or what we should do.

Have you ever felt so overwhelmed by different choices that you ended up doing nothing at all? That's what mental confusion can do. It's like standing at a crossroads with a hundred signs pointing in every direction. You want to make the right choice, but how can you when it's not clear which way is right?

This confusion isn't just something we feel inside. It spreads out into our communities like a cloud, making it hard for everyone to see clearly. When a whole society feels confused, it's like a ship without a captain, drifting without direction.

Why does this happen? Sometimes, it's because we get mixed messages. One person says one thing, another says something else.

And the media focus more on the back and forth debate, vs actually uncovering the truth. Who do we believe? It's like trying to follow a recipe where every ingredient is listed in a different language. How can we cook a good meal if we can't even understand the instructions?

In our fast-paced world, mental confusion is like a thick fog that rolls in without warning. It clouds our judgment, muddles our thoughts, and leaves us feeling uncertain and lost. This fog doesn't just affect one person; it can envelop entire communities, making it hard for us to see where we're going together.

Have you ever been in a group where no one can decide what to do? Maybe you're trying to pick a place to eat, but everyone has a different opinion. The conversation goes in circles, and in the end, you're all so confused and hungry that you just grab a bag of chips and call it a night. That's mental confusion on a small scale. Now, imagine that in a whole society. It's like a city full of people who can't decide where to go for dinner, so everyone ends up going home hungry.

This confusion can come from having too much information. It's like when you're trying to watch a movie, listen to music, and read a book all at the same time. You can't enjoy any of them because your attention is split. In our society, we're bombarded with news, opinions, and advertisements all day, every day.

How can we make clear decisions while you're looking at your phone, pretending to have a conversation with someone, and realizing you haven't understood a word they've said. Imagine this small interaction, happening a thousand times in your own community every hour, every day, whether it's a living room, a coffee shop or an office.

Do you think people 20 years ago might have had a bit more focus and clarity when making important societal decisions?

And then there's the issue of who to trust. It's like if you asked five different people for directions and they all pointed you in different ways. You'd stand there, scratching your head, wondering if you should just stay put. In society, we have leaders, experts, celebrities, and friends all telling us what to think and do. But what if they don't agree? Who do we listen to?

Mental confusion can also make us doubt ourselves. It's like when you're taking a test, and you second-guess every answer. You knew the material yesterday, but now, under pressure, you're not so sure. In society, this self-doubt can make us hesitant to act. We might have a good idea about how to improve our community, but the confusion makes us keep it to ourselves.

But it's not all bad news. We can cut through this confusion. It starts with focusing on one thing at a time. It's like when you're cleaning your house. If you try to do everything at once, you'll get overwhelmed. But if you start with just one room, you'll make progress.

In the past ten years, we were trained to think that multitasking was a powerful skill to have, but in recent years, every psychological authority has essentially admitted that it's impossible for a mind to effectively execute multiple complex tasks at the same time.

Now, business advice and productivity gurus almost unanimously advise training one's 'deep focus', the ability to shut out additional stimuli and focus on completing one task at a time.

We can feel and see in our own surroundings, how this lack of focus has made things worse, and causes us to accomplish much less, while at the same time, feeling more stressed and like we have no time at all.

So, what can we do right now to clear away the mental confusion in our society? We can start by simplifying things. Break down big problems into smaller, manageable parts.

We can start by being clear with each other. Say what you mean and mean what you say. Stop having a conversation with two people at the same time, one on your texts, and one in the same room.

And we can be patient, with ourselves and with others. It's okay not to have all the answers right away. It's like planting a seed. You need to give it time to grow.

We can also prioritize. When your phone battery is low, and you need to save power. You close all the unnecessary apps and just keep the essential one running. In society, we can focus on the most important issues and put our energy into solving them first.

And we can learn to be comfortable with silence. It's in the quiet moments that we often find clarity. It's like turning off the TV and the music and just sitting with your thoughts. In those moments, the confusion can start to settle, and the path forward can become more clear.

In the end, a society without mental confusion is like a clear day after a storm. The air is fresh, the sky is bright, and we can see for miles. It's a place where we can all move forward with confidence, knowing that even if we don't have all the answers, we're on the right path together.

## Sadness and Depression

As we reach the final example in this chapter, we turn to perhaps the most silent yet profound impact of trauma on society: the pervasive sadness and hopelessness that can settle like a heavy fog over communities and generations. This is not just about individual battles with depression; it's about a collective malaise that can stifle our very spirit, hindering growth and dimming the light of future aspirations.

Across the globe, we're witnessing an alarming rise in depression, a tide that is sweeping over young and old alike. To see it clearly, we need only to look at the youngest members of our society. From ADD and ADHD to depression and child anxiety and depression, we're seeing an uptick in issues that simply weren't prevalent a generation ago. And it feels as if we're going backwards, not forwards. It's almost unspoken, but in many ways, we feel that we're becoming less sophisticated, less educated, and less capable.

When you go to the airport and head to the magazine rack, what few decades ago felt like 10 or more scientific or research magazines, are now replaced by simply one or two, with the rest of the selection being more frivolous literature.

Why is this happening? Why is it that with every passing year, more and more people feel this profound sense of hopelessness? Is it the pressure of modern life, the isolation of our digital world, or the echoes of trauma that reverberate through our collective consciousness?

The impact of this widespread sadness is profound. When people lose hope, they lose the energy to strive for better. This lack of vision for the future can lead to a stagnation that affects every level of society, from the smallest village to the largest city.

But what does this mean on a day-to-day level? It means that projects go unfinished, because why bother? It means that talents go unexplored, because what's the point? It means that innovations go undiscovered, because who has the heart for it? And on a larger scale, it means that societies fail to thrive, because their citizens are too mired in despair to reach for success.

Yet, even in the midst of this sadness, there is a thread of resilience that runs through the human spirit. It's the part of us that, even in the darkest times, looks for a glimmer of light. It's the part that, even when burdened with sorrow, can still dream of joy. This resilience is our most powerful weapon against the tide of hopelessness.

So how do we combat this societal sadness? How do we nurture this resilience? It starts with connection. In a world that can feel so isolating, we must find ways to reach out to each other, to bridge the gaps that divide us. It's like joining hands to form a human chain, each person strengthening the next.

We must also create spaces where people can express their sadness without fear of judgment. It's like setting aside a plot in our communal garden for the flowers that bloom in the shade. These are the places where despair can be aired out and, in the sharing, begin to dissipate.

And we must foster hope. Hope is not a naive denial of reality; it's a defiant stand against despair. It's the belief that, even though the night is dark, the dawn will come. It's the conviction that, even though the path is steep, it is worth the climb. Hope is the seed that, once planted, can break through the toughest soil.

What can we do right now to bring hope back into our communities? We can start by recognizing the signs of sadness in those around us and offering a listening ear, a kind word, or a helping hand. It's like watering a wilting plant; sometimes, a little care is all it takes to bring it back to life.

Think of the last time you were in an elevator with a few people. Wasn't the mood horrible? The silence is deafening, and it feels like people don't know what to do with themselves for those few seconds of confinement with strangers. But if one person smiles, says a kind word, or even better, cracks a joke, the entire mood is lifted. It's like a huge weight has been released from the small elevator. And what did it take? Nothing - simply a person making an effort to be human (and a little bit of bravery).

Imagine these small pieces of effort happening wherever possible, over days, weeks, years, and a generation. It's not impossible to see how we could steer things back toward what many of us consider a more golden age in human interaction.

And certainly, one where people feel less isolated and depressed.

Indeed, trauma affects un individually, and as we've seen in this chapter, has massive repercussions on society at large.

Think about the times we've all faced something big, like a natural disaster or a pandemic, or a storm hitting a town. Some houses stand, some fall, but some are left with cracks that might not show until later. If we don't check on our neighbors, if we just clean up our own mess and move on, those cracks can grow. The next storm might do more damage because we didn't work together to repair what was weak.

And it's not just the big things. Daily life has its own traumas. The car that cuts you off, the rude comment online, the news of a distant war. They add up, like drops of water in a bucket. If we don't find a way to empty it, to talk about the little hurts and the big ones, the bucket might overflow.

In the end, it's about more than just seeing the trauma. It's about feeling it, knowing it's real, and doing something about it. It's about not letting the whisper of pain get lost in the noise of life. It's about making sure that when someone reaches out, there's a hand there to hold.

This book is a call to action. It's a reminder that we're all part of the same story, and every chapter matters. It's a promise that healing is possible, not just for one person,

r all of us, together. It's a journey into the heart of our
ᴧety, to find the trauma, to face it, and to heal it, one
person at a time.

# 8. A NEW DAWN: HEALING TRAUMA AND TRANSFORMING SOCIETY

As we reach the closing pages of our journey, it's time to reflect on the profound truths we've uncovered about trauma, the subconscious, and the path to healing. We've ventured deep into the human psyche, unraveling the intricate ways in which trauma not only affects individuals but also weaves its way into the fabric of society. It's been a journey of discovery, understanding, and hope.

## The Subconscious: The Hidden Driver of Our Lives

We've seen how our subconscious plays a crucial role in who we are and how we develop. It's like a vast ocean beneath the surface of our conscious mind, holding the secrets of our deepest fears, desires, and memories. Often, it's the uncharted waters of this subconscious that steer the ship of our life, sometimes leading us into storms we don't understand.

## Trauma's Ripple Effect Across Generations

Our exploration has revealed how trauma, when unprocessed, doesn't just stay with one person. It ripples out, affecting families, communities, and even entire societies. Like a stone thrown into a pond, creating waves that reach far beyond the initial splash. We've seen how unaddressed trauma can manifest in societal issues, from mental health crises to cycles of violence and addiction.

## Weighing Different Healing Methodologies

Throughout our journey, we've examined various methodologies for coping with and healing trauma. Like tools in a toolbox, each has its strengths and limitations. Some offer quick fixes, like band-aids for deeper wounds, while others, like psychotherapy, take a more gradual approach, peeling back layers over time. We've weighed these methods, understanding that there's no one-size-fits-all solution.

## The Promise of Real Solutions

Yet, amidst these varied approaches, we've discovered that real solutions do exist. Solutions that don't just skim the surface but go deep, addressing the root cause of trauma, and solving it. It's been an eye-opening realization over our years of experience that healing trauma is not just a distant dream but a tangible reality.

One of the most promising discoveries has been the potential of neuro-stimulus treatment. This natural process, has shown remarkable efficacy in treating trauma and addiction. It's like a key that unlocks the door to the subconscious, allowing individuals to confront and heal their deepest wounds.

## *The World Begins to Take Notice*

The world is slowly waking up to the potential of neuro-stimulus treatment. Yet, there's still much work to be done. We need to spread awareness, ensure safe and responsible use of these therapies, and integrate this powerful tools into broader healing practices. It's a path that requires courage, commitment, and collaboration.

## A Call to Action: Spreading the Word of Healing

As we close this chapter, we stand at the threshold of a new era. An era where healing from trauma is not just a personal journey but a collective mission. We have the knowledge, the tools, and the opportunity to make a significant impact on society.

Imagine a world where individuals are free from the chains of their past traumas. A world where communities thrive, unburdened by the weight of unprocessed pain. And a world where we can not only forgive those who have caused us suffering, but forgive ourselves from our guilt, shame, and fear. This vision is not just a hopeful dream; it's a possibility within our grasp, and we hope that the research in this book has demonstrated it clearly.

We invite you to join us in this mission. Spread the word that there is a solution to deeply rooted trauma. Share the stories of transformation and hope. Advocate for safe, accessible, and holistic approaches to mental health.

Together, we can create a ripple effect of healing that transforms not just individual lives but the very fabric of society. We can build a world where understanding, compassion, and healing are the cornerstones. A world where each of us, freed from the shadows of our past, can step into the light of our true potential.

As we turn the final page of this book, let's not see it as an end but as a beginning.

A beginning of a journey towards a healed, empowered, and transformed society.

We have identified the pathways towards happiness, hope and the kinds of friendships and personal relationships that enrich our lives and the lives of those around us. Through this, we can begin to see a future where unresolved trauma, along with its effects, does not have to be a life sentence.

The happy ending we're looking for is just ahead, and it's closer than we imagine.

# REFERENCES

Ambady, N. (2011) The Mind in the World: Culture and Brain. Association for Psychological Science, May 4, 2011

https://www.psychologicalscience.org/observer/the-mind-in-the-world-culture-and-the-brain

Psychotherapy Networker.

https://www.psychotherapynetworker.org/blog/details/1130/the-evolution-of-trauma-treatment

Janet P. Les Nervoses. Flammarion, Paris, 1909.

Google Scholar

Nicholas O. Rule, Jonathan B. Freeman, Joseph M. Moran, John D. E. Gabrieli, Reginald B. Adams, Jr, & Nalini Ambady. (2010) Voting behavior is reflected in amygdala response across cultures, *Social Cognitive and Affective Neuroscience*, Volume 5, Issue 2-3, June/September 2010, Pages 349–355,

Van der Kolk BA. The body keeps the score: Memory and the evolving psychobiology of posttraumatic stress. (1994) *Harvard Rev. Psychiatry* 1994; **1**: 253 265.

Van der Kolk, B. (2017) The Evolution of Trauma Treatment.

Van der Kolk, B. (2002) Trauma and Memory. Psychiatry and Clinical Neurosciences.

https://doi.org/10.1046/j.1440-1819.1998.0520s5S97

https://www.cedars-sinai.org/blog/science-of-kindness.html

https://ggsc.berkeley.edu/images/uploads/GGSC-JTF_White_Paper-Generosity-FINAL.pdf

"Who's Minding the Mind?" (Science Times, NYT, 7/31/07)

Made in the USA
Columbia, SC
03 February 2025

52351221R00083